CHILDREN'S CLOTHING

DESIGNING, SELECTING FABRICS, PATTERNMAKING, SEWING

Selma Rosen
Associate Professor & Assistant Chairperson
Fashion Design Department
Fashion Institute of Technology

FAIRCHILD PUBLICATIONS
New York

TO CARL ROSEN

Children's Illustrations by
MARNA BRENER

Diagrams executed by Karen Wiedman
Book Design by Elaine Golt Gongora

Copyright © 1983 by Fairchild Publications,
Division of Capital Cities Media, Inc.

All rights reserved. No part of this book may be reproduced in any form without permission in writing from the publisher, except by a reviewer who wishes to quote sources in connection with a review written for inclusion in a magazine or newspaper.

Standard Book Number: 87005-430-9

Library of Congress Catalog Card Number: 82-083319

Printed in the United States of America.

Third Printing 2005

F.I.T. COLLECTION

foreword

The publication of this book is wonderful news for the large numbers of young "to be" designers, teachers and mothers.

A book such as this has been needed for a long time. It offers in-depth details from start to finish on how to create a garment—nothing has been left out. One has but to pick up this book, start on page one, follow each step, and Voilà—a creation has been born. If this book was available when I started in the children's business, it would have saved me much grief and time. My background did not encompass patternmaking and I was not aware of the detail that was necessary for the creation of a new style. I was more involved in the styling of a garment rather than patternmaking and the detail involved. It would have been much simpler for me to have had Selma Rosen's book available rather than take a course in patternmaking. As a matter of fact, we intend to use her book in both our patternmaking and design departments, since I know it will be of great help to our staff.

Selma Rosen's background as both designer and assistant chairperson and instructor at F.I.T. give her all the proper credentials to write this book. Having worked with her at F.I.T., I know how well versed she is in this field. We have employed several graduates from F.I.T. in our design department. We find that after being trained by people such as Mrs. Rosen and other members of the F.I.T. staff, they have a more practical knowledge of the working world.

Again, I recommend this book highly to designers, teachers, mothers, and professional people in our industry.

Ruth Scharf
President, Ruth Scharf Ltd.

foreword

Here is the ideal book for those who want to create clothing for children. Professional techniques are simply and clearly presented so that they can be followed by just about anyone, beginners learning basic methods and pros with extensive sewing experience. All will find here helpful instructions in all phases of the design and construction of children's wear.

Professor Rosen has brought to this book her years of experience as a designer and teacher. Her methods of patternmaking and sewing for children's wear are totally professional. Her effective presentation of the material has been developed during many years of working with students in the children's wear classes at F.I.T. Many of these students have gone on to become successful designers in today's children's wear industry.

It has been my pleasure to work closely with Professor Rosen in the children's wear area of the Fashion Design Department at F.I.T. Her competence as a designer and instructor have earned her the respect of both colleagues and students. This book—complete and comprehensive from the selection of fabrics to the finished garment—attests to her thoroughness and dedication to excellence.

Hilde Jaffe
Dean, Art and Design
Fashion Institute of Technology

preface

The inspiration for **Children's Clothing: Designing, Selecting Fabrics, Patternmaking, Sewing** came from my students in the children's wear major classes at the Fashion Institute of Technology. I have tried to outline for the novice designer, as well as for the more advanced designer, many of the basic concepts used in children's wear design, patternmaking, and garment construction. This book will introduce a system of designing, patternmaking, and sewing that has been used for years by the garment industry.

Happily, designing children's clothes is not a difficult task. The best designs for children are the simplest—those that have simple shapes and feature one or two really good design elements. An additional bonus to designing clothes for children is that many of the problems of fitting adult clothes never arise. You are dealing with a small figure that is fairly straight and flat, which makes fitting garments (a very important part of the final result) comparatively simple.

Having lots of creative ideas, however, is only the first step in making children's clothes. You also need a means of translating those ideas into garments.

You are creating original designs and that means adapting the general instructions discussed in this book to your specific needs. Use these instructions as a guide. You may, at times, have to combine more than one method because of the design features in your special garments. As in any area of creativity, you will necessarily be breaking new ground. Being a designer means not only creating the original idea, but following through to the finished garment. The follow-through can be as challenging as the original design.

The book is divided into five units. The first unit deals with how to go about planning the design, selecting slopers and fabrics, and laying out your pattern in fabric. Sketches throughout the book should help to stimulate your imagination in planning the design. The second unit will explain how to properly fit the garment to your child. Unit Three shows you how to make the slopers you will need to execute your designs. You will learn—step-by-step—exactly how to use the slopers to make the paper patterns for your own designs. The fourth unit of the book is devoted to sewing individual parts of the garment as well as sewing the garments together. Here is where you will learn how to turn out really professional-looking clothes. All the sewing techniques you'll need to construct a successful garment are included—from sewing seams to making pretty pinafores with ruffles. Unit Five will discuss any additional trimmings or details needed to finish your garment.

Making children's clothing is an exciting way to express your creativity and the benefits are many. As a professional designer, there is almost always work in the children's wear industry. Parents will always need to buy clothing for growing children. As a hobby, making clothes for your (or someone else's children can be fun and wonderfully satisfying.

Selma Rosen
New York
1983

contents

UNIT ONE
GETTING STARTED 1

Tools & Supplies for Patternmaking 2
Tools & Supplies for Sewing 3
All about Slopers 5
   Selecting the Correct Sloper Size 6
   Measurement Chart 7
   Determining Finished Lengths for Garments 7
First Comes the Design 8
Selecting Fabrics 12
   Prints & Patterns 13
   Napped Fabrics 13
   Interfacing 14
   Trimmings & Notions 14
Determining Yardage Required for Garments 15
   Yardage Equivalency Chart 15
   Remnants 15
Grainlines 16
Basic Patternmaking Instructions 18
   Shortening the Sloper 21
   Lengthening the Sloper 21
Laying Out & Cutting Patterns in Fabric 22
   Preparing the Fabric 22
   Pattern Layout 23
   Layout Regarding Special Fabric Problems 25

UNIT TWO
FITTING CHILDREN'S CLOTHING 26

Fitting Skirts 27
Fitting Pants 27
Fitting Dresses, Jumpers, Shirts, Blouses 28

UNIT THREE
PATTERNMAKING FOR CHILDREN'S CLOTHING 29

Drafting Necklines 30
Drafting Facings 34
   Drafting Neckline Facings 35
   Drafting Armhole Facings 35
   Drafting One-piece Neckline & Armhole Facings 36
   Drafting Facings for Openings 37
Openings & Closings 39
   Zippers 40
   Buttons & Buttonholes 40
Drafting Collars 42
   Drafting Round Collars 43
   Drafting Basic Peter Pan Collars 44
   Drafting Cape Collars 44
   Drafting Bertha or Puritan Collars 45

Drafting Straight-line Collars	46
Drafting Convertible Collars	47
Drafting Mandarin Collars	49
Drafting One-piece Shirt Collars	50
Drafting Sleeves	51
Drafting Basic Long Sleeves	52
Drafting Short Sleeves with Shaped Bottoms	53
Drafting Puffed Sleeves with Band Cuffs	54
Drafting Puffed Sleeves with Self Ruffles	55
Sportswear	56
Drafting Yokes	58
Gathers	60
Drafting Blouses with Straight Yokes	63
Pleats	64
Inverted Pleats	64
Box Pleats	66
Side Pleats	67
Drafting Blouses	68
Drafting Shirts	71
Drafting Vests	72
Drafting Skirts	73
Drafting Dirndl or Gathered Skirts	75
Drafting Flare Skirts	77
Drafting Wraparound Skirts	78
Drafting Jumpers	80
Drafting Jumpers with Scoop Necklines & Front Pleats	81
Drafting Jumpers with Shoulder Openings	82
Drafting Jumpers with Lowered Waistlines	83
Drafting Pants	84
Drafting Boxer Pants	85
Drafting Fly-front Pants	86
Drafting Fly-front Pants with Trouser Pockets	87
Drafting Waistbands for Skirts or Pants	89
Drafting Suspenders for Skirts or Pants	91
Drafting Suspenders with a Bib	92

UNIT FOUR
SEWING CHILDREN'S CLOTHING   93

Basic Sewing Instructions	94
Pressing	95
Seams & Seam Finishes	95
Stitch Size	96
Sewing Plain Seams	96
Sewing French Seams	97
Sewing Flat-felled Seams	98
Sewing Intersected Seams	98
Sewing Facings	99
Sewing Shaped Neckline Facings	99

Sewing Back-opening Facings for Buttons	100
Sewing Back-opening Facings for Zippers	101
Sewing Armhole Facings	102
Sewing One-piece Neckline & Armhole Facings	103
Sewing Facings for Buttoned Shoulders	104
Sewing Collars	105
Sewing Peter Pan Collars	105
Sewing Peter Pan Collars with Trimmings	105
Sewing Peter Pan Collars with Collar Binding to Garments	107
Sewing Mandarin or Band Collars	108
Sewing Convertible Collars	109
Sewing Two-piece Shirt Collars	110
Sewing Sleeves	111
Sewing Puffed Sleeves with Band Cuffs	111
Sewing Sleeves with Bias Binding	112
Sewing Sleeves with Trimmings	112
Sewing Sleeves with Self Ruffles	113
Sewing Sleeves with Cuffs	113
Sewing Faced Placket Openings	114
Sewing Continuous Placket Openings	115
Sewing False Placket Openings	116
Sewing Sleeves with Linings	117
Sewing Sleeves into Garments	118
Sewing Yokes	120
Sewing Shirts	121
Sewing Skirts	123
Sewing Pants	124
Sewing Boxer Pants with Elastic Waistline Using Method I	124
Sewing Boxer Pants with Elastic Waistline Using Method II	125
Sewing Pants with Fly-front Openings	126
Sewing Pants with One-piece Front Zipper Closing	126
Sewing Pants with Trouser Pockets	128
Sewing Pants with Front Waistband & Elastic Back	129
Sewing Waistbands	131
Sewing Casings for Elastic	133
Sewing Hems	134
Sewing Buttons & Buttonholes	135
Sewing Snaps	136
Sewing Zippers	136
Sewing Slot for Centered Zipper	136
Sewing Seams for Lapped Zipper	137

Inserting Zipper into Slashed Opening on Woven Fabrics 138
Inserting Zipper into Slashed Opening on Knit Fabrics 140

UNIT FIVE
ADDITIONS & TRIMMINGS 141

Ruffles 142
   Ruffles on an Inside Seam 143
   Ruffles with a Heading 143
   Pinafore Ruffles 144
   Ruffles at Neckline & Armhole 144

Piping & Binding 145
   Preparing Bias Strips 145
   Joining Bias Strips 146
   Single Binding 146
   French Piping 146
   Finishing Binding & Piping 147
Cording 147
String or Spaghetti Ties 148
Appliqué & Embroidery 149
   Machine-made Appliqué 150
   Handmade Appliqué 150
Belts & Sashes 151
Pockets 154
Flaps & Tabs 156
Metric Conversion Table 157

UNIT ONE
GETTING STARTED

tools & supplies for patternmaking

- *Paper*

Professional patternmaking paper is ideal, but it is only available in very large rolls. A good substitute is white shelf paper taped together to produce large sheets. Brown kraft paper is another good alternative. Avoid using newspaper because the newsprint can rub off on the fabric.

- *Rulers*
1. L-square (preferred)
2. 2" by 18" clear plastic ruler

- *French Curve or Armhole Curve*

- *Pencils*
1. #2 (soft) pencils, sharpened
2. Red or blue colored pencils to make corrections on patterns

- *Scissors*

Any old or blunt pair (cutting paper with fabric scissors will dull them).

- *Table*

A large flat surface to work on such as a cutting board or cork-top table

tools & supplies for sewing

- *Sewing Machine*
- *Scissors*

6 to 7 inches long, well sharpened

- *Ironing Board and Iron*
- *Tapemeasure*
- *Pins*

Straight pins—not too heavy (#17 satin pins are best)

- *Sewing Needles* (and *Thimble* if you prefer to use one)

- *Dressmaker's Tracing Paper*
- *Tracing Wheel*
- *Loop Turner* (not necessary, but good to have handy)
- *Cutting Board or Cork-top Table* (not necessary, but good to have handy)

all about slopers

The *sloper** is a *master pattern,* usually in a basic shape that has been very carefully constructed for size and fit. Patternmakers and designers use slopers to make paper patterns of original designs which will subsequently be cut in fabric and sewn into garments.

The sizes of the slopers in the package are 2, 4, 6, and 8. The sizes 3, 5, and 7 have not been discussed because adjusting the fit as you sew is comparatively simple. Children's figures are flat and straight and since they tend to grow more in the length than in the width between sizes, adjustment is often minimal.

You can see the versatility of using slopers in the designs throughout this text. All the garments can be made from the basic slopers using the correct patternmaking techniques. Once you have mastered the use of slopers, you can create original designs.

1. Cut out a set of slopers in the size you plan to use. You can make a complete set or choose individual sections for your garment. Paste each section onto heavy paper or oaktag. This will help to preserve them so they can be used over again.
2. Accurate and clearly drawn lines are very important. Remember that the *lines you draw on your paper will ultimately be the seams you will sew in fabric.* The finished garment will reflect the accuracy of your lines.
3. Use a *ruler* or *L square* as a guide when drawing straight lines. Use the *French curve* when drawing curved lines. All lines should be continuous and blended. It is easier to sew lines that do not bump or break suddenly.
4. Slopers *do not* have seam allowance. Seam allowance is a small amount of fabric (½″) that is used for sewing the garment together. Slopers *do not* have hem allowance. Hem allowance is an amount of fabric, usually 1″ to 2″, added to the bottom edges of the garment such as a skirt, blouse or sleeve to finish it.

    Seam and hem allowances can be measured directly onto the fabric when the paper pattern is laid out for cutting. You can

---

*The slopers referred to in this text are available in a separate package called *Master Patterns for Children's Clothing.* The package contains the basic slopers needed for the patternmaking of many types of clothing.

add the hem and seam allowances to the paper pattern if you prefer. However, if you make changes in the pattern such as cutting it apart for yokes, you will have to copy each section onto another piece of paper and measure the allowances.

selecting the correct sloper size

To determine what size sloper to use for your garment, it is desirable, whenever possible, to measure the *child*. Measurements should be taken with a tapemeasure.

CHEST Measure around chest, under the armpits at the widest point.

WAIST Measure at the natural waistline. Since young children lack a definite shape, it is sometimes difficult to determine the placement of a child's waistline. However, it normally falls approximately halfway between the shoulders and the beginning of the legs.

HIPS Measure around the buttocks at the widest point.

NECK TO WAIST LENGTH Measure from the base of the neck to the waistline at center back.

WAIST TO ANKLE LENGTH Measure from waistline to the ankle at the child's side.

Using the Measurement Chart, find the size closest to the child's measurements. If the measurements fall between two sizes, use the larger-sized sloper; making clothes slightly larger for children is usually good planning.

SIZE	2	4	6	8
CHEST	21"	23"	25"	27"
WAIST	20½"	21½"	22½"	23"
HIPS	21½"	23½"	25½"	28½"
NECK TO WAIST	8½"	9½"	10½"	11½"
WAIST TO ANKLE	19"	23"	27"	32½"

MEASUREMENT CHART

determining finished lengths for garments

DRESSES Measure the child at center back from *base of neck* to desired finished length.

SKIRTS Measure the child at center back from *waistline* to desired finished length.

PANTS Measure the child from waistline at the side seam to desired finished length. Long pants generally end at the ankle, but there are a variety of styles and lengths varying from shorts to knickers.

Adjust sloper as necessary. All lengths may be shortened or lengthened at the hemline.

first comes the design

There are four main steps to follow in order to complete a garment:
1. *Planning* the original idea or design.
2. *Making* the paper pattern.
3. *Cutting* the pattern in fabric.
4. *Sewing* the fabric into a finished garment.

The professional designer draws inspiration from many sources. Very often the fabric is a prime factor in developing an idea. Certainly if you see a pink and white checked gingham fabric, it will give you one idea, and a navy blue velveteen another. Trimmings also set the creative juices flowing. Color is, of course, a vital part of the designer's world.

Magazines, literature, movies, television, the whole world is full of design ideas which can become inspiration for your designs. Children's drawings and their ideas about the type of clothing they would like to wear also can help you in planning a garment. Think of the fun of adding an appliqué on a playdress or suit that a child helped to create.

The type of clothing you are planning also helps you in creating original designs. For example, if you are thinking about party clothes for girls, you will use ruffles, bows, and party-type fabrics and colors. If playclothes are what you have in mind, then be bold and lively in your choice of color and design.

There is hardly any distinction between fabrics for boys' and girls' garments, especially in playclothes. Generally, heavyweight fabrics such as denim, chino, twill, corduroy, and gabardine are bottomweights and are most suitable for pants and skirts. Lighter weight fabrics, such as chambray, poplin, gingham, and lightweight plaids for shirtings, are considered topweights. Knit fabrics also come in different weights, with single knits best suited for tops and double knits working well for both tops and bottoms depending on the yarn and construction.

You can begin to plan your first design by referring to the sketches in this book or in newspaper or magazine ads. Select the figure from the illustrations on the facing page that most closely resembles the size of the child for whom you are planning a garment. Place some tracing paper over the illustration and try out some ideas. Do several sketches—after awhile some ideas will look better to you than others. You might

GETTING STARTED/FIRST COMES THE DESIGN

rickrack or eyelet edge trim for neckline and sleeve edges

ribbon for neckline bow

zipper

back

front — *plain fabric or ribbon for center front panel / to be topstitched on dress center front*

like the neckline from one design and the sleeve or pocket from another. If this is your first attempt, choose a design that looks simple. The fewer changes you will have to make on the sloper, the easier the construction of the garment will be.

Draw your design on a piece of paper and keep it in view *at all times* (especially when you are working on your slopers).

1. Draw a front and back view of the garment.
2. Indicate where the closing will be. Show buttons and buttonholes or zipper, on front or back.
3. Make notations on the sketch so that you will know what trimmings and notions will be needed.
4. *Be sure* you read and understand the unit on PATTERNMAKING in this book before you begin your project. The unit covers each phase of patternmaking needed to complete your design. You should have a complete set of patterns assembled before you start to lay out the pattern on the fabric. For example, you will need the following set of pattern pieces for the dress sketched above.

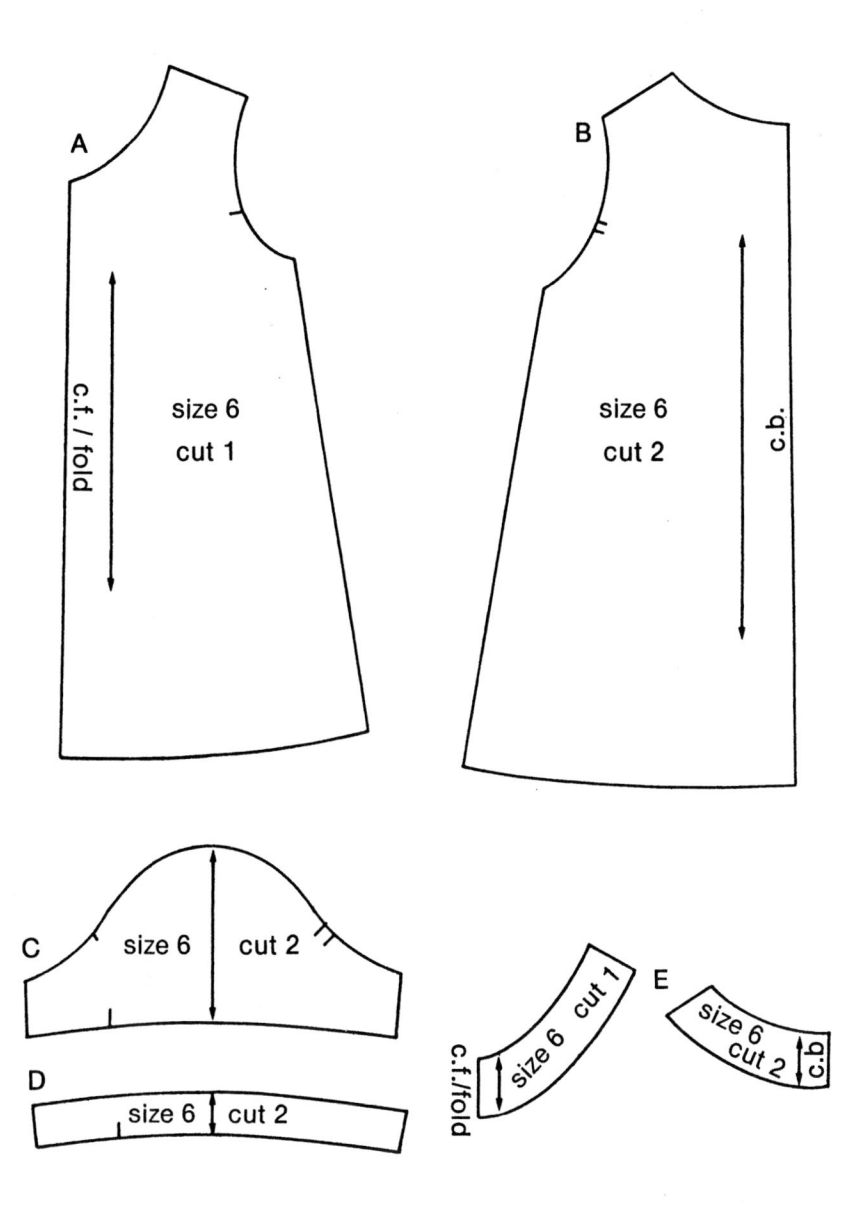

A. One front dress pattern (basic sloper with scoop neckline).
B. One back dress pattern (basic sloper with scoop neckline).
C. One sleeve pattern (basic long sleeve, which is shortened and shaped at the bottom).
D. Facings or bias strip for sleeve finish.
E. Facings or bias strip for neckline finish.

selecting fabrics

Fabric is a fabulous source of inspiration to a designer. There are countless fabrics on the market suitable for making children's clothing. Not only are there fabrics made from a variety of natural and man-made fibers to choose from, but also varieties of weaves, finishes, colors, and patterns as well. The choices are dazzling!

Fabric begins with fibers, the material from which yarn is spun, and it may be woven or knitted. Fibers can be natural, such as cotton, linen, wool, and silk or man-made such as polyester, nylon, and acrylic. Some fabrics are made of all natural fibers, some of all man-made and some of combinations of natural and man-made.

The yarns are woven or knitted into many different types of fabric, from very lightweight such as lawn and organdy to heavy corduroys and double knits, with a huge range of options possible. The more you look at fabric the more you come to realize the many possibilities.

Cotton and cotton blended with man-made fibers are probably the most often used fabrics for children's wear. Usually sturdy and easy to care for, cotton and cotton-blends come in many varieties and are often priced lower than wool, silk, or linen. Denim, chambray, chino, gingham, organdy, piqué, poplin, and voile are some of the terms you will see in cotton fabric displays.

When selecting a fabric, it is important to consider the style and type of garment that will be made. For example, a dress with a full gathered skirt will need a softer fabric than an A-line skirt. An A-line skirt will need a fabric with some body so that it will not fall limply. A fabric ideal for a boy's playpants will not be ideal for his dress-up shirt.

Be selective in choosing a fabric. Consider the care requirements of the fabric you plan to purchase. One general rule that particularly applies to children's clothes is that they should be washable and durable. Children play hard and get dirty, whether they are boys or girls. Therefore, it is better to make the clothes "kid-proof" than to try and make the kids clothes-conscious.

Sometimes if a fabric requires special treatment such as dry cleaning, it may be economical to buy a more expensive fabric that is easy to care for. There are, for example, many woolen fabrics on the market, but only some of them are machine washable and dryable. If these machine-washable woolens cost more initially, the added investment will be offset by avoiding dry-cleaning bills.

Most cotton, cotton-blends, and many man-made fabrics are easy to care for. However, always check with the salesperson before the fabric is cut from the bolt. If more than one fabric is to be used for the same garment, make sure *they* are *compatible*. A washable garment that is trimmed with a non-washable fabric or trimming cannot be laundered successfully.

prints & patterns

Patterns in fabrics also influence the selection of fabrics. Print fabrics make great looking children's clothes! Used alone or in combination with solids or other prints, they show less dirt and wrinkles than solids. There are also many prints especially made for children.

When choosing prints, plaids or stripes, try to keep in mind the size of the child you are making the garment for. Very large prints or patterns tend to dwarf a small figure. Small patterns generally work better, especially on toddler and small children's size ranges. Sometimes, however, a creative designer can use a fabric not particularly designed for a child's garment and do something very innovative, using imagination and taste.

Most prints come in allover patterns which means the pattern pieces can be laid up or down on the fabric. However, some prints have a one-way design and will have to be cut in one direction. Checking the fabric carefully is important because one-way fabrics will require approximately one-half yard of additional fabric. A border design, printed along the selvage of the fabric, is an example of a one-directional design. Garments made from border prints are cut on the crosswise grainline of the fabric in order to take advantage of the border print.

napped fabrics

Fabrics such as corduroy, velveteen and brushed denim are napped fabrics. Corduroy and brushed denim are sturdy fabrics that wear well and have a pleasant feel to the hand. These fabrics are heavier and generally warmer and make good fall and winter garments. Velveteen is a good choice for holiday and party clothes. It has a luxurious look and feel, but is made of cotton or a cotton and man-made blend of yarns.

Uncut corduroy looks and feels like velveteen but wears like corduroy and makes excellent playclothes.

Napped fabrics "shade off" or look different depending on the direction the fabric is held. Napped fabrics must be cut in one direction *only* and garments will require additional yardage.

interfacing

Interfacing is a woven or nonwoven fabric used to face certain parts of a garment to add body. Some interfacing materials include Pellon®, Siri®, Sibonne®, perqueline, and lawn. These materials are available in different weights and with different fiber contents. If the garment is washable, buy a washable interfacing. Most fabric stores can advise you regarding the best type of interfacing to use for a particular fabric and garment.

trimmings & notions

It is a good idea to buy the necessary trimmings and notions for your garment when buying the fabric. Thread, zipper or buttons, and trimmings can be matched accurately and you will have everything you need at hand when you begin sewing.

Trimmings, such as appliqués, eyelet embroidery, lace, rickrack, braids and a variety of edges, are excellent ways to vary the design of a garment. A very basic dress or blouse which has a trim added to the collar, hem or front can become an entirely original creation. Trimmings can also be used to accentuate or define style lines. Appliqués and embroidered patterns can be used on boys' clothing as well.

determining yardage required for garments

Fabric is woven or knitted in widths ranging from 36" to 72". Most cotton and cotton-blends, however, run approximately 36" to 45" wide. One way to determine how much fabric to buy is to lay the pattern pieces out on a table, which has been marked to the *width* of the fabric you expect to buy. *Remember* the pattern pieces are only half of the garment and they will have to be cut double. Therefore, plan as if the fabric is folded in half, selvage to selvage. *Be sure* to observe the grainlines of the pattern pieces. Grainlines should run parallel to the selvage where a lengthwise grainline is indicated. This method will give you a good approximation of the yardage needed.

When you get to the store, however, you may find a fabric in a different width from what you had estimated at home. Use the Yardage Equivalency Chart to help you convert your yardage to what will actually be required.

Fabric Width	36"	39"	45"	54"	60"
Yardage	1 5/8	1 1/2	1 3/8	1 1/8	1
	1 7/8	1 3/4	1 5/8	1 3/8	1 1/4
	2 1/4	2 1/8	2	1 3/4	1 1/2
	2 5/8	2 1/2	2 1/4	1 7/8	1 3/4
	3 1/8	3	2 3/4	2 1/4	2

YARDAGE EQUIVALENCY CHART

remnants

Remnants are cuts of fabric left on the bolt after most of the fabric has been sold. They are usually small cuts—a natural for children's clothing.

These cuts are generally reduced in price, because of their limited amounts.

Be careful about buying unidentified remnants. Try to find out what types of fibers are used and how to care for them. No matter how inexpensive the fabric is, it is not a bargain if it falls apart after the first washing.

grainlines

Woven fabrics are composed of yarns that run up and down and another set of yarns that interweave and run across the fabric. The yarns that run up and down are called the *lengthwise grainlines* and the yarns that run across, the *crosswise grainlines*. The lengthwise grainlines run parallel to the selvage. The *selvage* is the finished edge on either side of the fabric.

Clothes always hang better on the body when the fabric is used correctly. The fabric used lengthwise has different qualities than the fabric

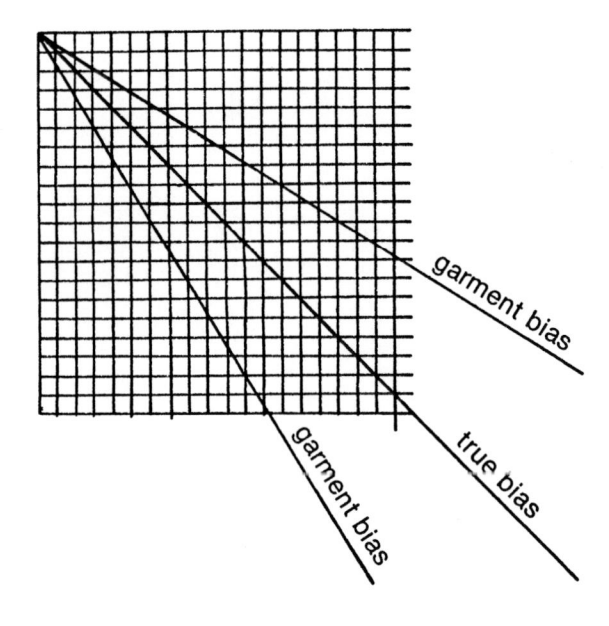

```
          selvage
    ┌─────────────────┬─────
    │                 │\
  cross              │ \  true
  grain              │  \  bias
    │                 │   \
    │  length grain   │    \
    └─────────────────┴─────
                      cross grain
          selvage
```

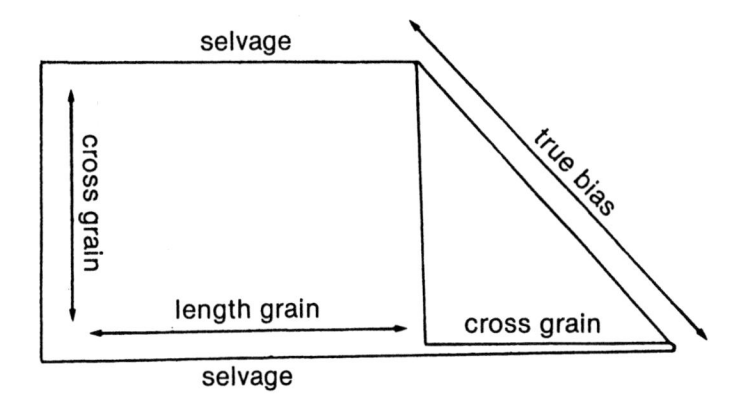

used crosswise. Therefore, it is important to be able to determine the grainlines of the fabric. Most clothes are made so that the lengthwise grain runs from neckline to hemline. There are some exceptions such as when a desired pattern is printed in a way that requires the use of the crosswise grain up and down.

In addition, there is a third way to use woven fabric—the *bias*. Any part of the fabric that is neither length grain nor cross grain, but falls on a diagonal, is called a *bias*. The bias also has special qualities that make it useful. It tends to stretch more than the straight grains and can be used to this advantage by the sewer.

A line that exactly bisects the length and cross grains is called the *true bias*. The true bias on the fabric can be determined by folding the cross grain to the length grain exactly line to line. Fabric cut on the true bias has the most stretchability of woven fabrics and is always used for areas that require a close or contoured fit such as for binding, pipings, and other trimmings. A line that is not exactly true bias, but is still a diagonal, is called a *garment bias*. The garment bias is not suitable for bindings or pipings, but can be used in other ways, such as for a flared skirt.

Knitted fabrics do not have length and cross grains. Knitted fabrics are formed by looping one loop of yarn into the next. Knitted fabrics can be knit in a circular manner, which produces a tubular fabric. Tubular knitted fabrics are generally cut apart before laying out a pattern. Other knits are flat and resemble woven fabrics on the bolt. Depending on the type of yarn and knitting process used, the fabric will stretch in one or two directions. Knitted fabrics always have more stretch than woven fabrics.

basic patternmaking instructions

1. Prepare a piece of paper that is approximately 4" longer and 4" wider than the selected sloper. Using a ruler, draw a straight line 2" away from the left edge of the paper.* Line should be slightly longer than the sloper from neckline to hem.

2. Align the center front (or center back) of the sloper with the line on the paper. Sloper edge should touch line. Using a sharp pencil, outline sloper carefully. Try to reproduce the original as closely as possible.

With a sharp pencil point punch a hole at the top and bottom of the grainline.

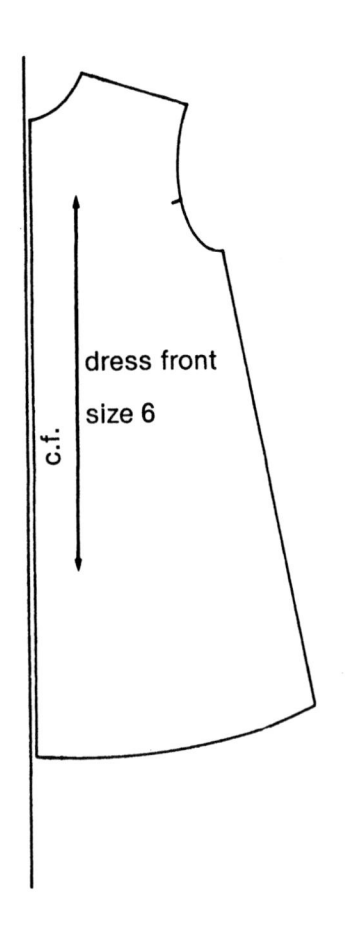

dress front

size 6

c.f.

*When drafting sleeves or pants, draw line on the center of the paper and align straight grainline of sloper on the line.

3. Remove sloper. Using a ruler or French curve as needed, true* sketched lines. When using the French curve move it around the neckline until the curve follows the sketch line exactly. Repeat at armhole trying whenever possible to draw the curve in one continuous line (this may not always be possible).

4. Label *center front* (or *center back*) line. If line is to be placed on fold indicate as such. Label size and pattern section. Draw in straight grainline.

5. Use this paper sloper to draw in your style lines. Refer to your sketch and to the appropriate patternmaking section in this text for instructions on individual areas of the garment.

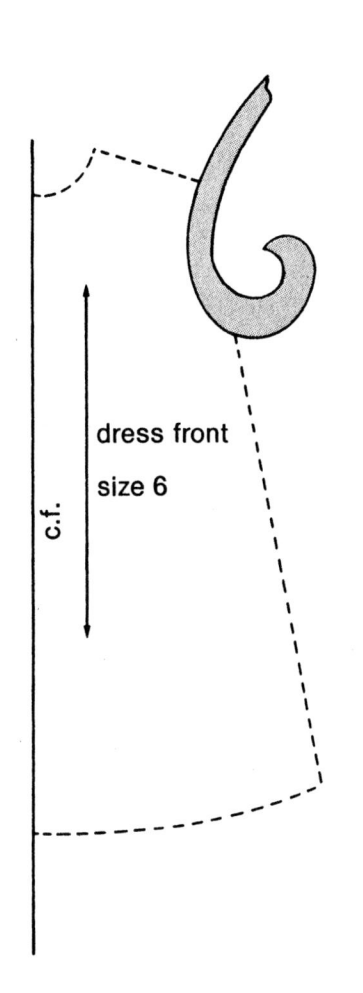

dress front
size 6

c.f.

*Trueing lines means to form one continuous line using a curve or a ruler as a guide. The *trued line* then becomes the pattern *sewing line*.

6. *Crossmarks* or *notches* are used on sections of the sloper which are to be separated. Crossmarks help in the accurate reassembling of the pieces after they have been cut apart.

Crossmarks must be added before the pattern is cut apart. Each section is labelled and straight grainlines, centers, and foldlines, if any, are indicated.

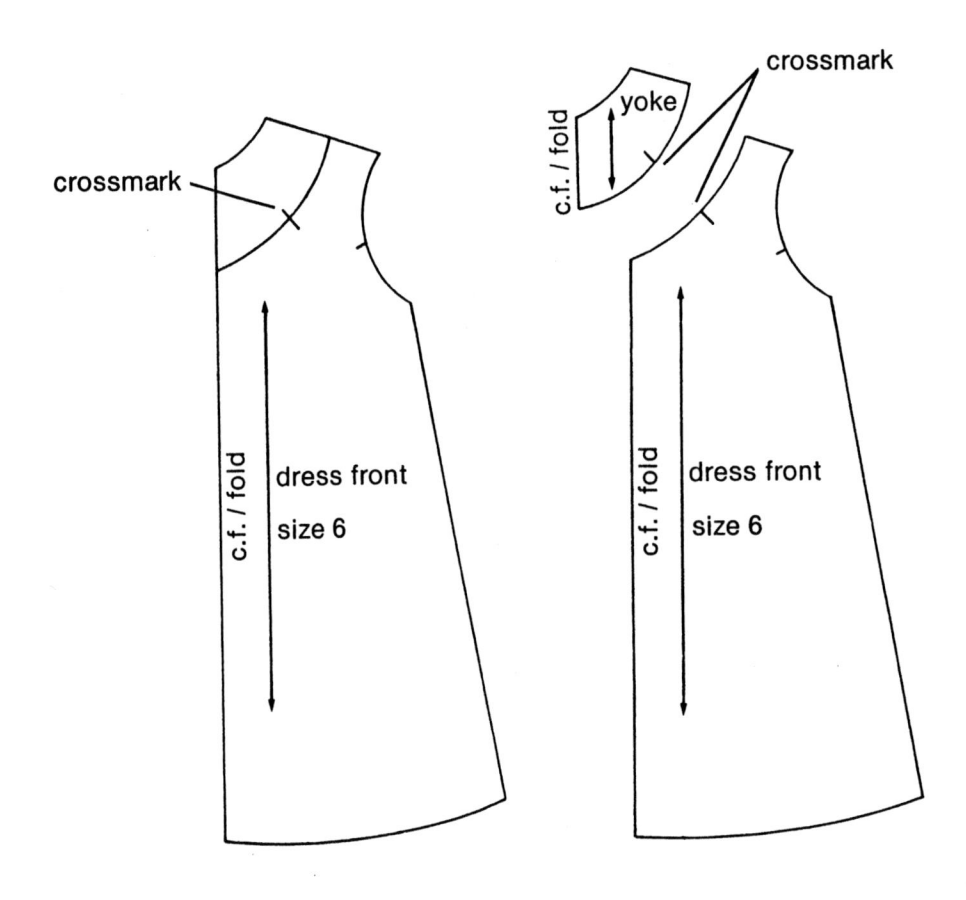

shortening the sloper

To shorten the sloper measure up evenly at hem edge the desired amount. Draw a line that follows exactly the shape of the hem edge. Repeat on back sloper.

Use this method to shorten pants, skirts, and shirts.

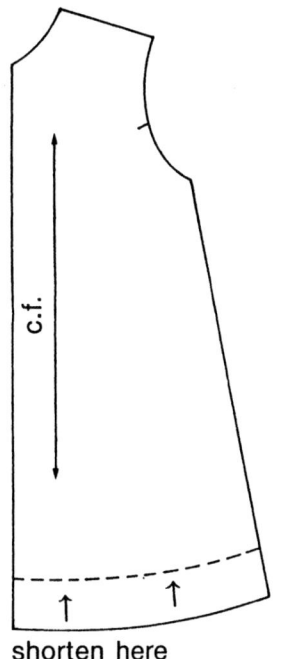

shorten here

lengthening the sloper

To lengthen the sloper extend center line and side seamline with a ruler. Measure down the desired amount and true as discussed above. Repeat on back sloper.

Use this method to lengthen full-length and/or midi-length dresses and skirts.

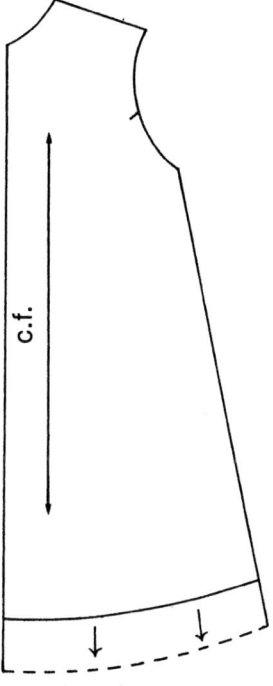

lengthen here

laying out & cutting patterns in fabric

Complete the entire set of patterns for your design before beginning the layout. Check and label each pattern piece, if you haven't done so already. Be sure you are aware of which pieces will need to be cut on a fold at the center and which will have a seam and seam allowance at the center. *Grainlines must be clearly indicated on each pattern piece.*

preparing the fabric

Woven fabric will sometimes be finished in a way that causes the grainlines to be pulled awry. For the very best results with any garment you make, the fabric must be properly prepared.

1. Clip the fabric at the selvage and tear across the fabric to the opposite selvage. If the fabric has a fancy weave or heavy threads running through, use the *pulled thread method* discussed below. Plain woven fabric will usually tear very easily.

PULLED THREAD METHOD Straighten the crosswise end of woven fabric by clipping the selvage and carefully pulling one crosswise thread. The fabric will pucker and you can cut along the line of the thread (pucker) from selvage to selvage. Repeat on the other end of the fabric.

2. Fold the fabric in half. The edges should line up squarely. If they do not, then the fabric is off grain and will have to be pulled into shape.

3. Pull the fabric on the diagonal or bias where it is short. Very large cuts may need two people to pull a short end. Some fabrics straighten quite easily. Others, particularly permanent-press fabrics are very resistant and can never be properly squared.

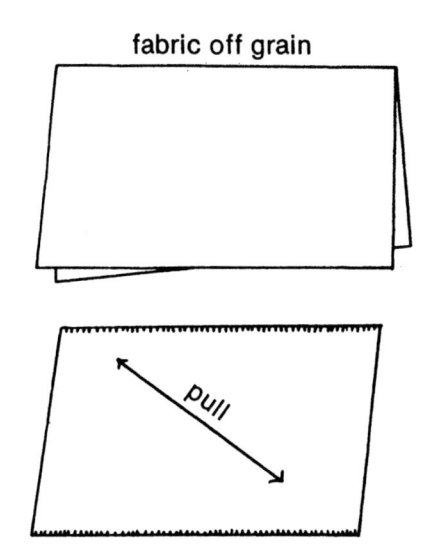

Sometimes printed, stripe or plaid fabrics are printed offgrain and even when the grains are straight the fabric still looks offgrain. In that case follow the printed *pattern* rather than the *grainlines*.

Always fold fabric with the right side or face of the fabric inside. Do all markings such as seam allowance on wrong side of the fabric.

pattern layout

For garments with a main pattern piece cut on a fold at the center, and the other main piece with a seam at the center, fabric can be folded in half, selvage to selvage. Pattern pieces may be placed side by side if fabric is wide enough. Be sure to leave sufficient space between pattern pieces to measure seam allowance around each piece as needed. (If seam allowance has been added to paper patterns, patterns can be placed closer together.)

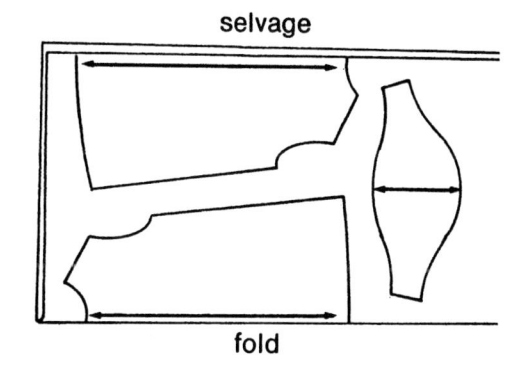

To cut a garment with two main pattern pieces on a fold at the center back and center front, fold fabric in a *gate fold*. Bring both selvages to the center of the fabric. If necessary, after cutting these pieces refold fabric to cut other pieces.

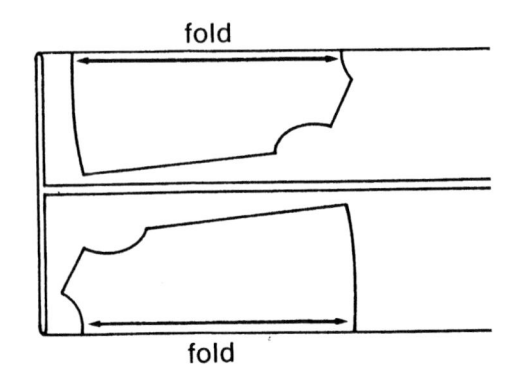

Remember once you have cut the fabric you cannot go back. Check the following list before cutting fabric:

1. Measure grainlines where indicated from selvage or fold.

2. Leave enough space between pattern pieces if seam allowance has to be added to the fabric.

3. Measure seam allowance very carefully where needed.

4. Account for all pattern pieces.

5. Cut accurately on seam allowance lines. Clip crossmarks not more than ¼" into seam allowance. *Do not* clip too far.

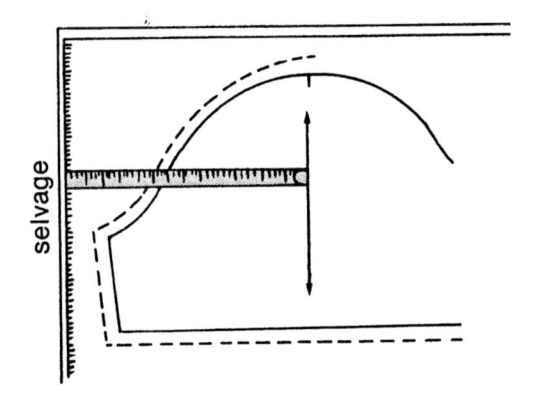

layout regarding special fabric problems

PLAID FABRICS Plaid fabrics will require matching when the pattern is laid out. The pattern pieces where the seams are joined should line up neatly on the cross grainlines of the plaid.

When laying out plaids, draw the plaid design onto the paper pattern at the crossmarks on the side seam and/or the hemline. This method can be used for any area of the garment that needs to be matched, *except* when pieces are cut together such as at a center seam.

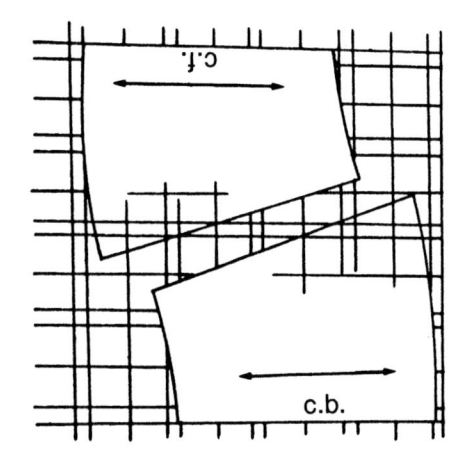

NAPPED FABRICS As discussed previously, napped fabrics such as velvet, velveteen, corduroy or brushed denim "shade off" or look different in opposite directions. By holding the fabric up first one way and then the other, you will see the difference in color. You can then decide which look you prefer—with the nap or against the nap. Whichever direction you decide, *all* pattern pieces must be laid out and cut in *this* same direction.

KNITTED FABRICS Some knits will also look different when cut in different directions. Hold up opposite ends of the lengthwise grain of the knit fabric to determine if the fabric needs to be cut in one direction.

PRINTS WITH ONE-WAY & BORDER DESIGNS Some prints have a one-way design and will have to be cut in one direction. Check the fabric carefully so that the design will not be standing on its head on parts of the garment. One-way designs require approximately one-half yard additional fabric.

A border design is printed along the selvage of the fabric and is another example of a one-way design. Garments made from border prints are cut on the crosswise grainline of the fabric in order to take advantage of the print.

UNIT TWO
FITTING CHILDREN'S CLOTHING

It is not difficult to fit children's garments. If you have been buying children's clothing you know you can make purchases without having the child try on the garments, and that they usually fit. Most adjustments which need to be made are in the garment's length, rarely in the width.

A child's garment should fit comfortably—not so loose that it hangs limply and not so tight that it binds. You can eliminate a great deal of fitting and alterations by choosing the correct size sloper. Plan to sew garments that fit the child well when the garments are new rather than sew the garments *big* and have the child grow into them. Usually by the time the child grows into them, the clothes look old and shabby.

fitting skirts

1. Choose size of skirt sloper by child's waistline measurement. If waistline measurement falls between two sloper sizes, select larger size and take in side seam as needed. Plan waistband to child's waistline plus 3/4" for ease.

2. Shorten or lengthen skirt same as for sloper (see page 21).

fitting pants

1. The waistline on children's pants is elasticized and can be adjusted by tightening or relaxing the elastic.

2. Shorten or lengthen pants legs same as for sloper (see page 21).

fitting dresses, jumpers, shirts, blouses

After the garment has been cut and marked, remove the paper pattern.

1. Sew shoulder seams of garment.

2. Complete sewing the neckline in the desired style. The finishing of the neckline at this point is very important because the neckline will tend to stretch when the garment is fitted on the child. Many disasters can be avoided by finishing it first.

3. Baste or pin side seams together and try garment on child, pinning the opening together, front or back center over center.

4. Check the side seams. There should be about ½″ ease when side seam is held together (or 2″ all around). If more ease exists, take in the side seam until ease is not more than ½″ for front and ½″ for the back on each side seam.

UNIT THREE
PATTERNMAKING FOR CHILDREN'S CLOTHING

Creating patterns for original designs using slopers is patternmaking (or drafting). Most manufacturers of children's clothing use this method, because it is quick and very reliable. If the master pattern or sloper fits well, all garments constructed from these slopers should also fit as well.

Patternmaking (or drafting patterns) for children's clothing does not usually involve very complicated procedures. Working on the small figure necessarily limits the concepts that can be incorporated into one garment. As a designer, mastering the basic patternmaking techniques can be an invaluable tool.

drafting necklines

Whenever you plan for a neckline other than the basic high round neckline of the sloper, the best results are obtained when the front sloper is pinned to the model form or child. It is difficult to judge the proportion of how high and how wide the neckline should be while the sloper is on the table.

Use *one-half* of the *front sloper*. Hold the sloper up to the model form or child and adjust so that the armhole and neckline are in the proper position.

Sketch, very lightly with a pencil, the approximate shape of the neckline desired.

1. Place the sloper on a flat surface. Square sketched line at center front for ¼" with L-square. (This ensures a continuous line when garment is cut out on the double.)

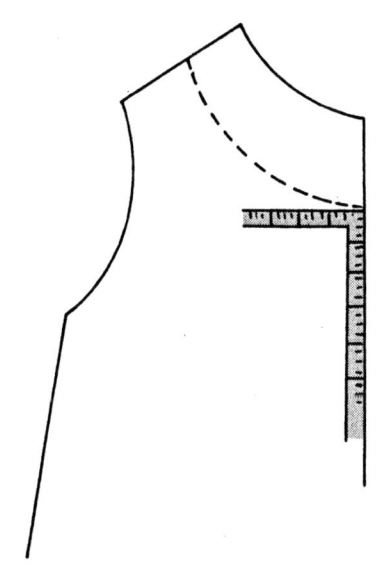

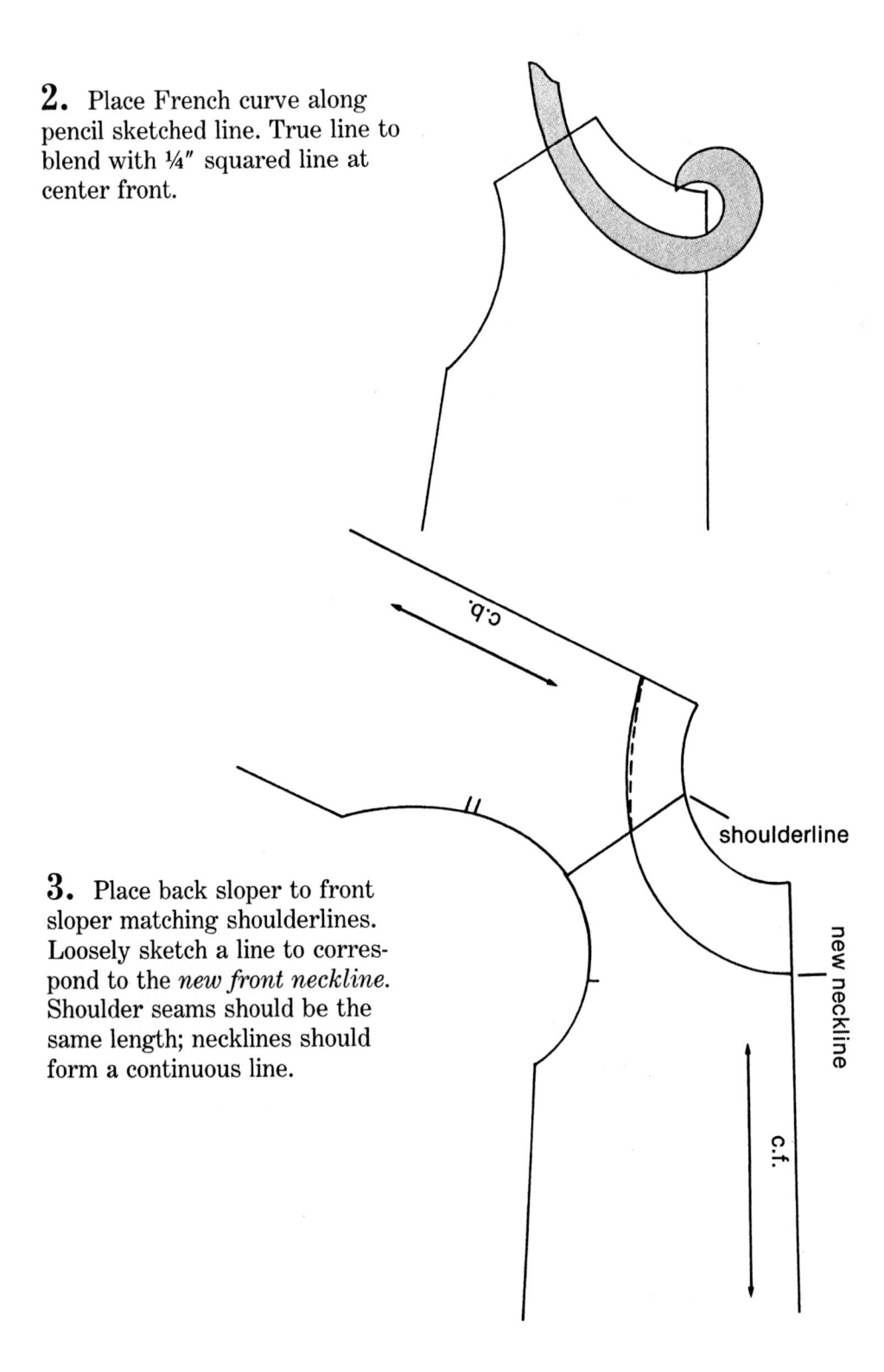

2. Place French curve along pencil sketched line. True line to blend with ¼" squared line at center front.

3. Place back sloper to front sloper matching shoulderlines. Loosely sketch a line to correspond to the *new front neckline*. Shoulder seams should be the same length; necklines should form a continuous line.

To true back neckline, follow instructions as for front (using an L-square or a French curve as the line requires). Cut along new neckline.

4. The shape of the neckline can vary according to your design. The tools for trueing the neckline will also vary, but the method can be adapted to any neckline design.

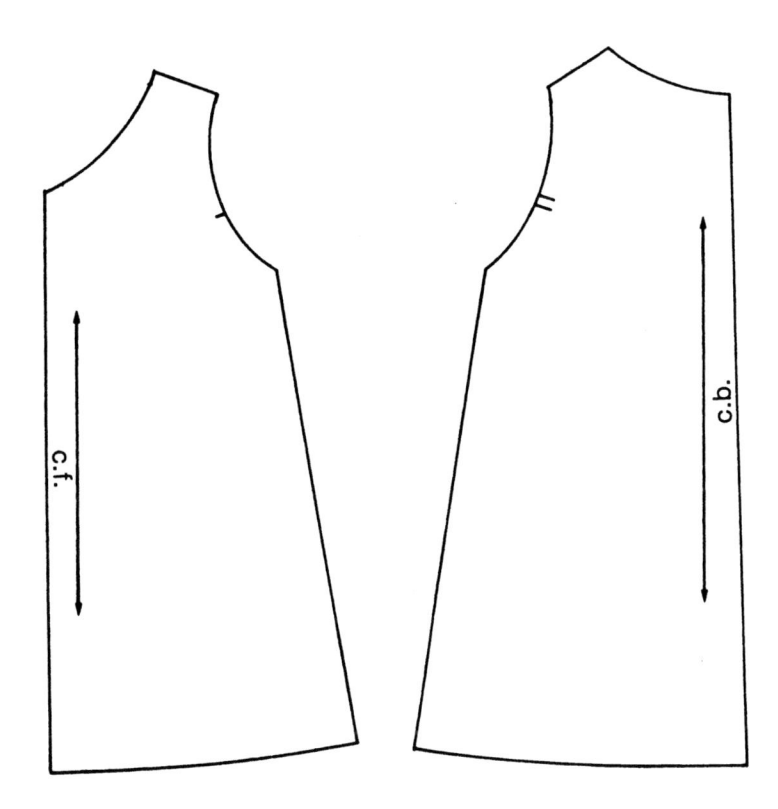

drafting facings

All outside edges of garments require some type of finishing. *Facings* are one way to finish a garment. Other methods include binding, piping, lining, and turning of hems.

Whenever the bottom edge of an area is shaped in such a way as to make turning up of a hem impractical, a separate facing is used as a finish. Facings are used on necklines, bottom edges of sleeves, jackets, vests, dresses, and pants.

A facing is an exact reproduction of the area edge to be finished. Facings fall into three basic groups: *shaped, bias,* and *extended.*

Note: Broken lines indicate inside facings.

drafting neckline facings

Necklines can be finished with collars, bindings, pipings, or facings. The decision as to how a neckline should be finished depends on the style, fabric, and general use of the garment. Neckline facings are often shaped.

1. Complete neckline design as desired.

2. Copy neckline, shoulder, and center front lines.

3. Measure down from neckline about 2" evenly all around. Mark center front and grainline. Grainline of the facing will always be the same as the grainline of the garment section to be faced. Mark grainline on facing.

4. Repeat facing procedure for the back neckline. Cut out facing patterns.

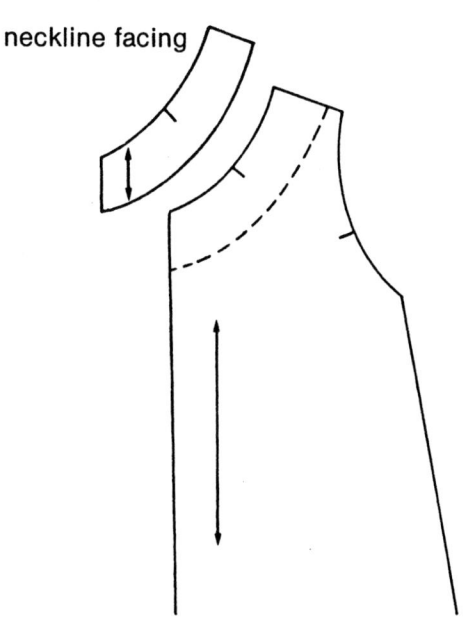

drafting armhole facings

1. Copy shoulder seam, armhole, and side seam of pattern.

2. Measure in from line 1¼" to 2" depending on style of garment.

3. Repeat procedure for back armhole. Measure grainline of main pattern piece to facings. Cut out facing patterns.

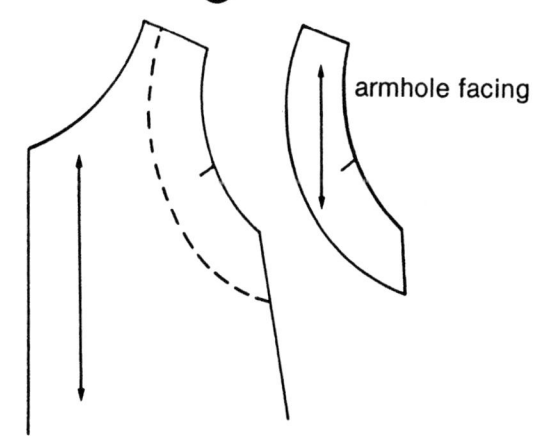

drafting one-piece neckline & armhole facings

When a garment requires a neckline and an armhole facing, a one-piece facing which incorporates both facings can be drafted.

1. Follow instructions for neckline facing copying the entire shoulder seam, armhole, and part of the side seam at the same time.

2. Shape the bottom of the facing by measuring down at center front and at the side seam approximately 1½ to 2". Draw a gently curved line from center front to side seam. Mark grainlines.

3. Repeat for back.

4. Cut out all facings.

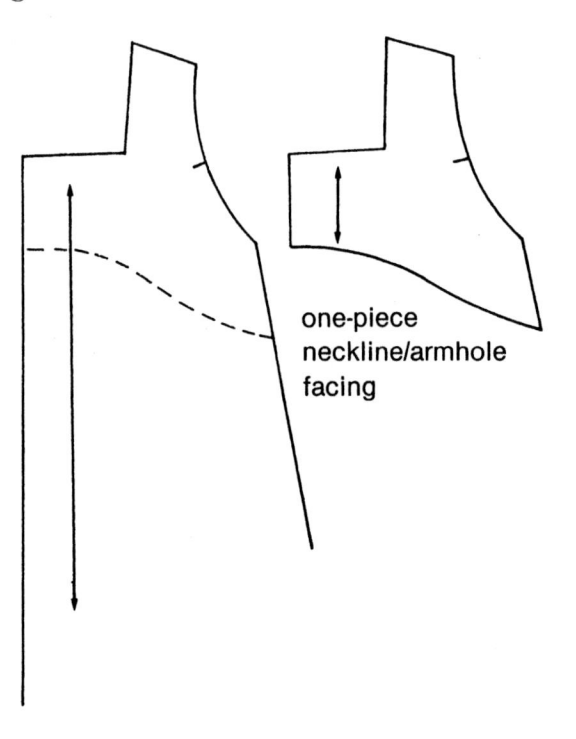

one-piece neckline/armhole facing

The preceding method of drafting a facing can be applied to any neckline shape or any garment area that requires a facing. The width of the facing may vary depending on the section of the garment being faced. For example: on a scalloped sleeve bottom 1½" may suffice. However, on the front of a jacket a 3" to 4" facing may be needed.

drafting facings for openings

When planning a garment with a front opening for buttons and buttonholes or for a zipper, which may be worn open or closed at the neckline, it is desirable to have a clean finish on the inside, especially in the neckline area. This is achieved with a facing that continues from shoulder seam around the neckline down to the bottom of the opening.

The facing for this type of neckline can be made all-in-one (a fold-back facing) with the front of the pattern or as a separate facing which is sewn on. Less fabric is required for a separate facing.

FOLD-BACK FACING

1. Copy pattern on a piece of paper approximately 10" wider than the pattern. Add an extension line to center front. (See BUTTONS & BUTTONHOLES to determine width of extension.)

2. Fold paper back on extension line and trace neckline and 1½" to 2" of shoulderline. Measure approximately 2" to 3" at bottom edge of pattern. Blend a curved line from shoulder to hem.

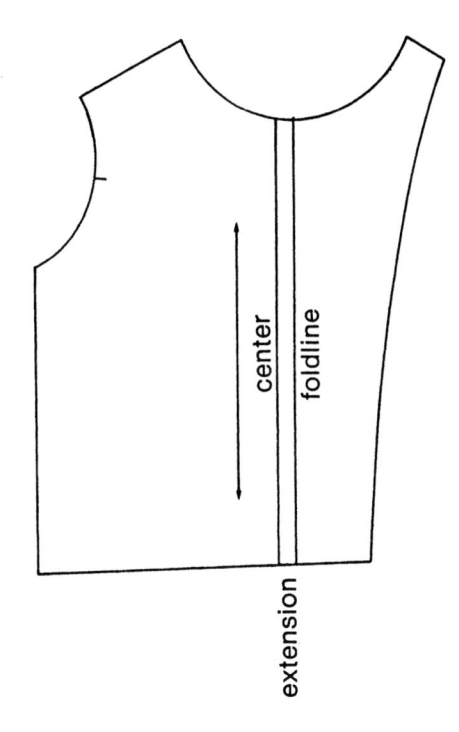

SEPARATE FACING

When a separate facing is planned, place pattern to be faced on a separate piece of paper and draft as for FOLD-BACK FACING. Add seam allowance at extension edge.

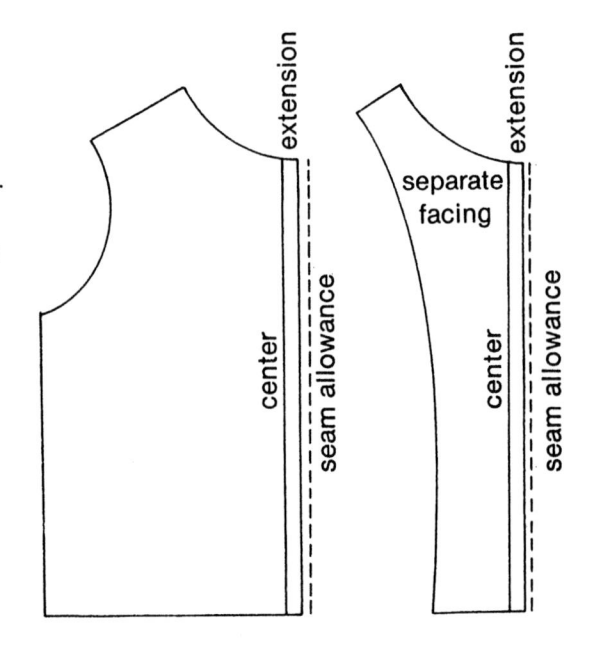

Openings which close up to the neckline such as for back buttons or for front buttons, can take a simple 3" fold-back facing. Fold paper back on extension line and trace part of the neckline. Draw a straight line down to the bottom of the garment.

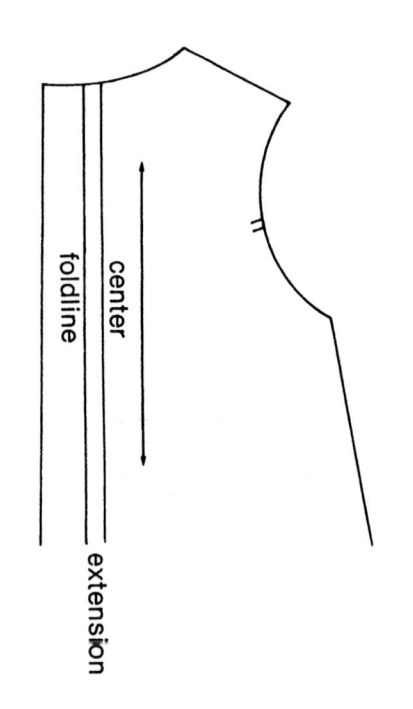

openings & closings

Most garments, unless they are made of stretch knit fabric, need some type of opening to facilitate putting the garment on and taking if off. Dresses and tops need a neckline opening; skirts and pants, a waistline opening. Zippers and buttons and buttonholes serve this purpose most often.

When the opening is at the front of the garment, it is usually considered part of the design. Back openings are generally considered purely functional.

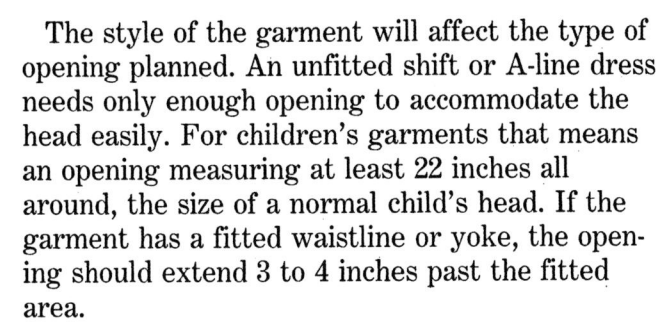

The style of the garment will affect the type of opening planned. An unfitted shift or A-line dress needs only enough opening to accommodate the head easily. For children's garments that means an opening measuring at least 22 inches all around, the size of a normal child's head. If the garment has a fitted waistline or yoke, the opening should extend 3 to 4 inches past the fitted area.

A skirt, which is open from waistline to hemline, would need an extension for buttons and buttonholes using the same method as for shirts.

A very important factor to remember when planning for openings and closings is that the *center* of a garment *never changes*. If the pattern needs to be adjusted to a larger or smaller size, the adjustment should be made at the side seams. The closing must bring the garment sections together as if there were *no* opening at all.

zippers

1. When planning for a zipper that is placed into a center seam, add ½" seam allowance to the pattern.

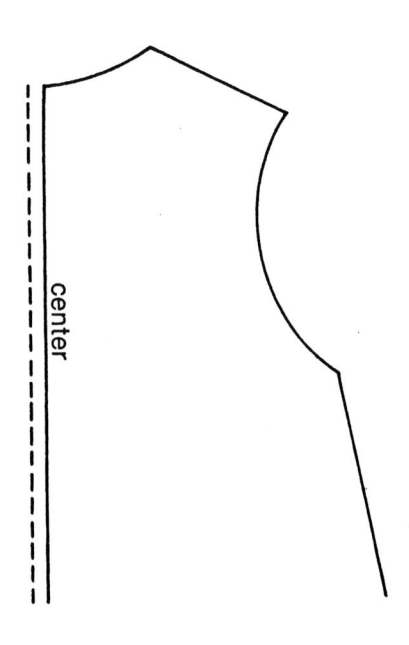

2. When planning a zipper for an area without a seam allowance, such as on the neckline of a blouse or dress, *do not* make any pattern changes. Mark the length of the zipper for a slash at the center back or center front.

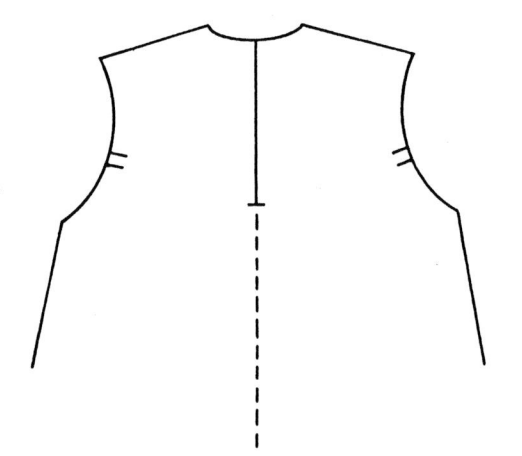

buttons & buttonholes

Buttons can be decorative and are sometimes an important design feature. Garments designed with buttons and buttonholes always need additional fabric to extend past the center line, so that when the buttons are buttoned they do not fall off the edge of the fabric. When the button is pulled through the buttonhole, it will slide over and half of it will be on the extension. The two center lines will meet on top of each other exactly. Buttons should be sewn *on* the center line.

The size of the extension depends on the size of the button. The extension will always be one-half the size of the button plus ¼" to ½" depending on the size of the button. For example, a 1-inch button will need a 1-inch extension—one-half the button size plus ½". However, for a ½-inch button, ¼" measurement added to one-half the button size is sufficient. You will have to use your judgment when you use smaller or larger buttons.

The number of buttons used on a garment depends on the size of the button. Buttons and buttonholes raise the cost of a garment and manufacturers never use more than is necessary to keep the garment closed.

PLACEMENT OF BUTTONS & BUTTONHOLES
Buttonholes which are placed *horizontally* from center line into the garment will hold the garment closed most effectively. Buttonholes can be made *vertically* when a band or tab is part of the opening. Placement for vertical buttonholes is directly on the center line.

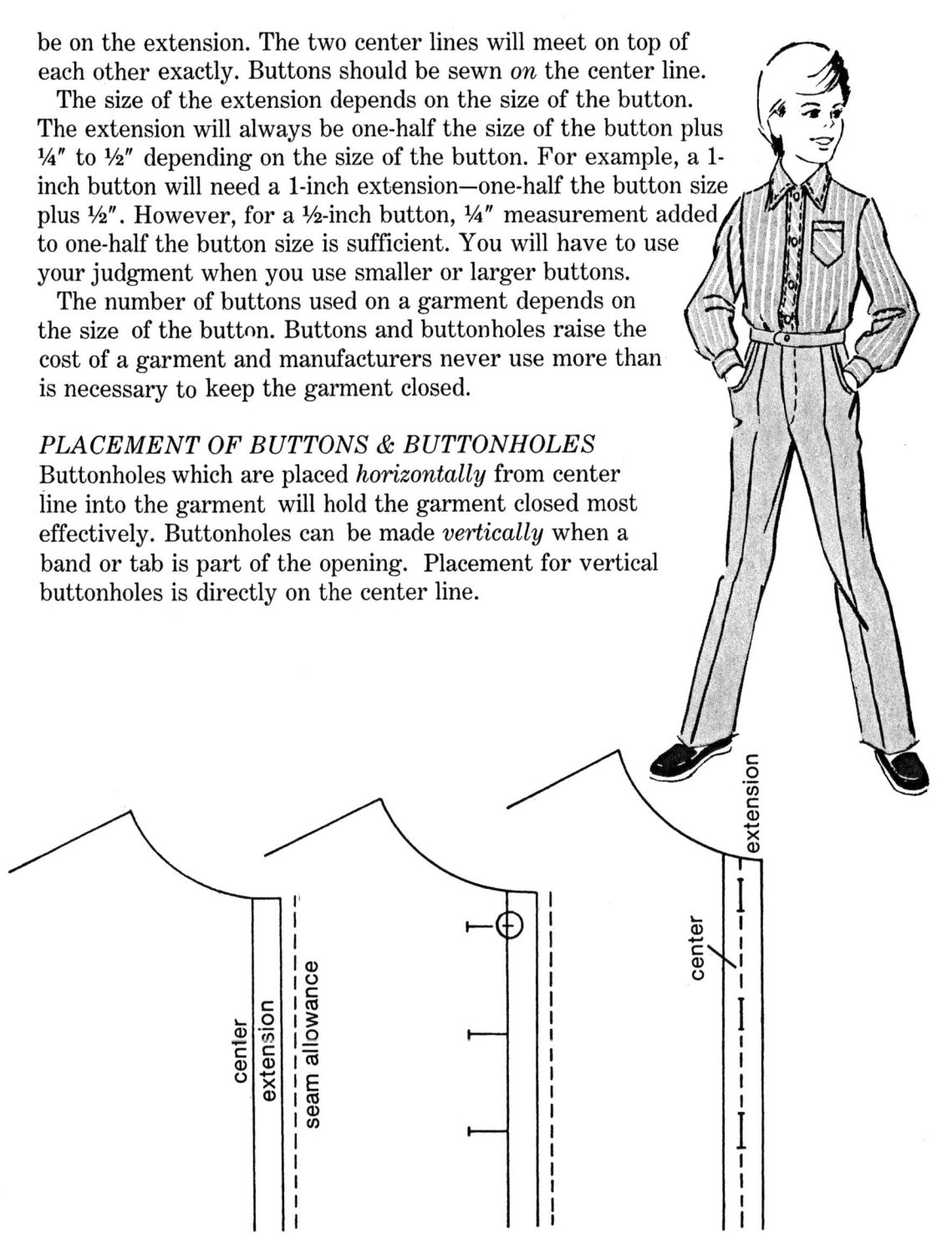

drafting collars

An important design feature on a child's garment is a collar. One reason is that a collar acts as a frame for the child's face and another because an interesting collar can change a garment from a simple one to a special one.

The classic children's wear collar is the Peter Pan. There are many variations on the Peter Pan collar such as the Bertha collar and the Puritan collar. Other collars important in children's wear are the Mandarin, the band, and the convertible or shirt collar.

An excellent way to vary the design of collars is to use trimmings. Eyelet edges, rickrack, ruffles, and embroidery set into the edge of the collar add interest and originality.

Collars fall into two main categories: *round collars* and *straight-line collars*.

Round collars conform to the rounded shape of the neckline and tend to follow the contour of the body. For example, the *Peter Pan collar*.

Straight-line collars are drafted from measurements and *do not* lie as flat around the neckline as round collars but tend to stand up more around the neck. For example, the *Mandarin collar*.

drafting round collars

1. *Do not* change the neckline shape of the dress sloper.

2. *Do not* change the neckline shape of the collar sloper. The collar will not fit properly when sewn.

3. *Do* change the outside contour of the collar sloper if desired.

4. Place the grainline of the collar either on the length or cross grain, depending on the fabric design and layout. However, the preferred grain is lengthwise at center back, especially if the center back is a foldline.

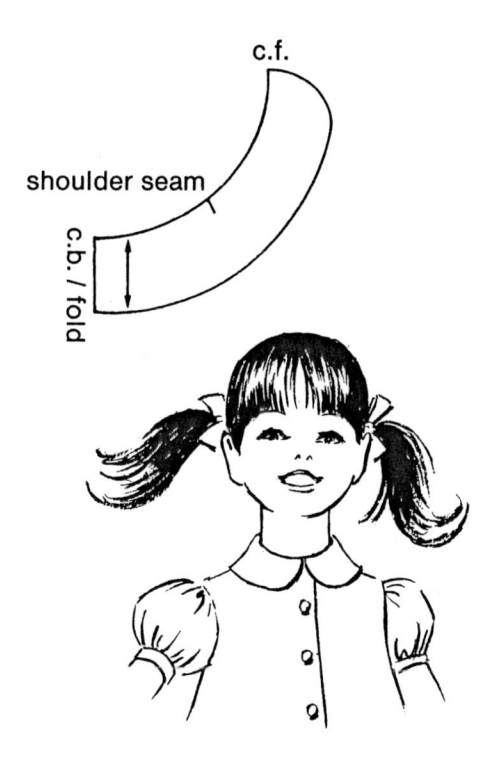

Use the *Peter Pan collar* sloper to develop the following collars.

1. The *basic Peter Pan collar* has a center-back fold and a rounded front. This shape is best for garments with front openings.

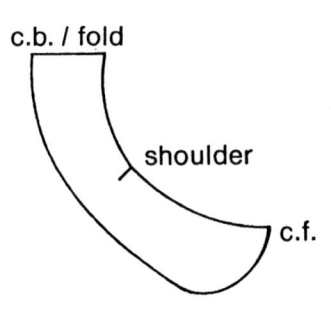

2. Collar can be split on the foldline and/or rounded for garments with back openings.

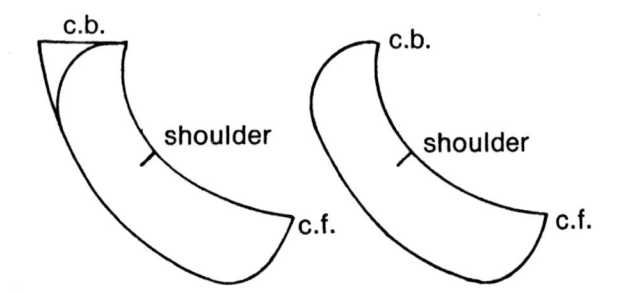

3. *Cape Collar*—use basic Peter Pan collar sloper; fold or split at center back depending on the style of the garment. Measure out from neckline of sloper desired width of finished collar evenly all around. Be careful that the proportion of the collar is in keeping with the size of the garment.

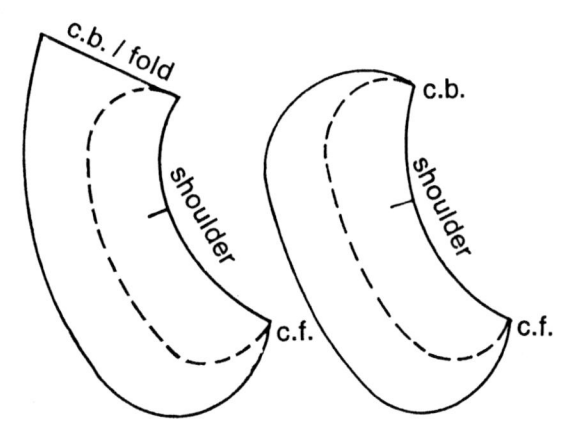

4. *Bertha or Puritan Collar—* one piece in front and split at the back. Place Peter Pan sloper on center front of dress sloper, matching neckline and shoulder crossmarks. Trace center front foldline from dress sloper. Then proceed as for cape collar reversing shaping with curve at center back.

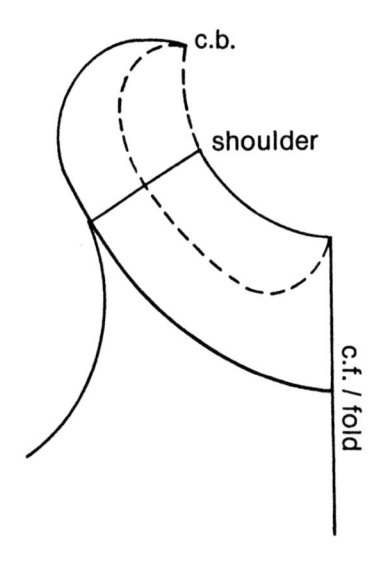

5. Outside edge of Peter Pan collar may also be fully or partially scalloped.

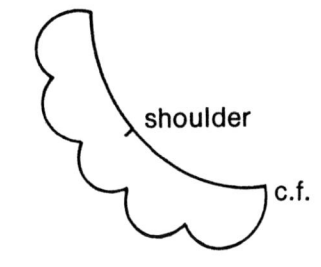

drafting straight-line collars

1. Straight-line collars stand up around the neckline more than round collars. The *convertible* or *shirt collar* stands up on the neckline at the center back and folds down on itself the amount of the stand. It lays flatter as it comes around to the front. The convertible collar can be worn open or closed at the front neckline.

The *Mandarin collar* stands up all around the neckline and usually has a curved shape at the center front where it meets.

2. Plan to use the *basic dress sloper* for the neckline measurements.

3. Measure the neckline curve of the sloper with a tapemeasure. Curve the tapemeasure around the neckline measuring from center back to shoulder and then from shoulder to center front. Hold tapemeasure so that the markings rest directly on the neckline for the most accurate measurements.

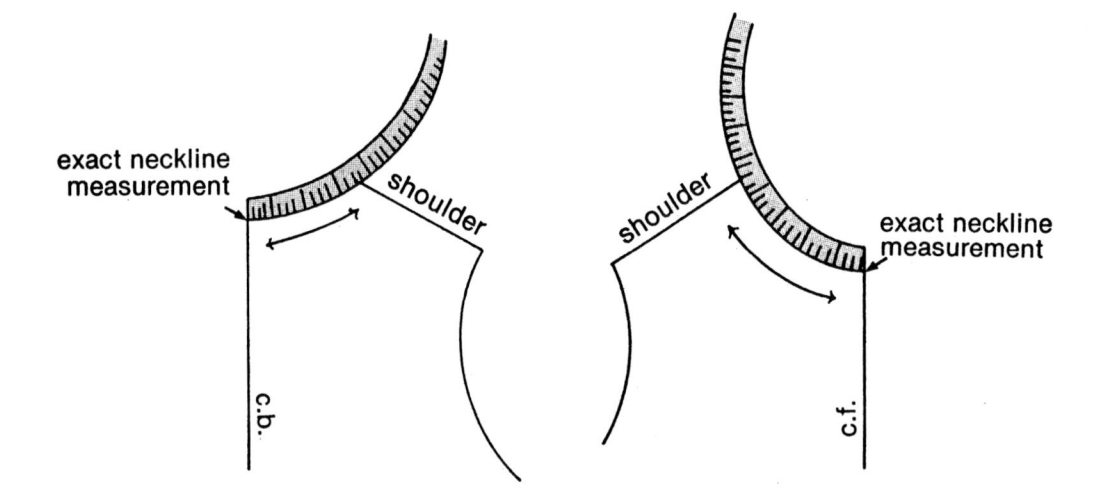

drafting convertible collars

1. Square a piece of paper about 3″ wider than the entire neckline measurement (double the measurement from the sloper) and about 5″ or 6″ long.

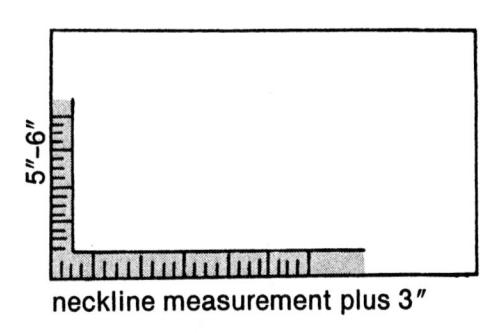

2. Fold width of paper in half.

3. Fold paper in half again lengthwise. Label *center back fold*.

4. Measure up from bottom edge ½″ and draw a line across paper. On this line, crossmark your measurement from center back to shoulder; then crossmark measurement from shoulder to center front. Measure up ½″ at center front and crossmark.

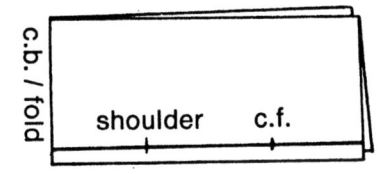

5. Using French curve blend a line from shoulder crossmark to center front crossmark.

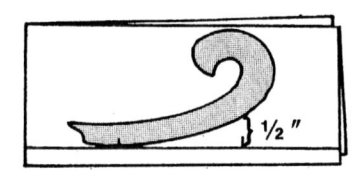

6. Square a line up from center front crossmark to folded edge of paper. This will be for a finished collar with a very wide spread at center front. Collar shape can be angled out from the center line to form a point for a more traditional collar.

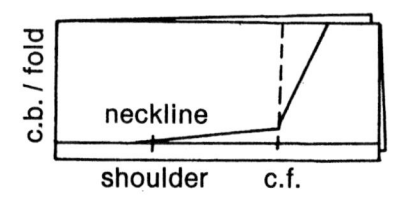

7. Transfer crossmarks to underside of paper. Cut out collar and open for completed pattern.

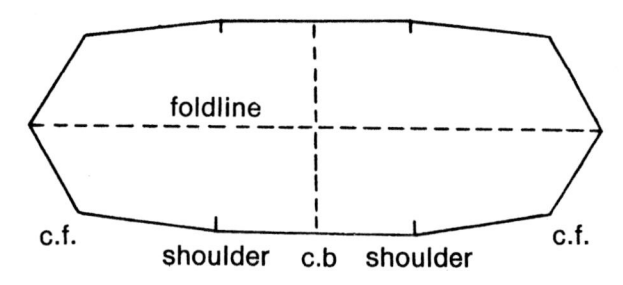

drafting mandarin collars

1. Square a piece of paper about 3" wider than the entire neckline measurement (double the measurement from the sloper) and about 3" long.

2. Fold paper as in Step 3 of convertible collar and follow Steps 4 and 5. Square up at center front to top edge of paper.

3. Measure up 1" to 1¼" at center back neckline and continue to measure evenly to center front. Complete collar by drawing a curved line at front edge of collar *slanting away* from center front line.

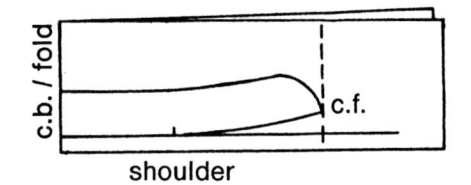

4. Transfer crossmarks to underside of paper. Cut out collar and open for completed collar.

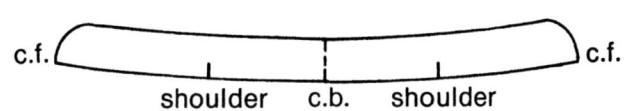

drafting one-piece shirt collars

1. Fold piece of paper 7" long and 3" wider than neckline measurement in half. Draft Mandarin collar.

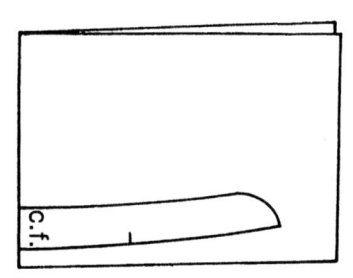

2. Following curve at center front, draw a straight line up to top of curve. Shape a line up and out from this point at the same angle as below. (Width of collar should be ½" wider than band.) Draw a curved line to center back fold.

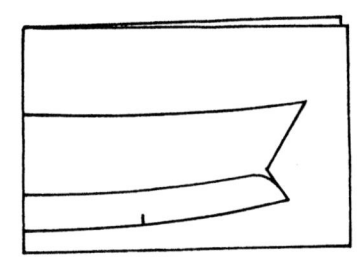

3. Measure out at center front an amount equal to the shirt extension for buttons (about ½"). Draw a curved line.

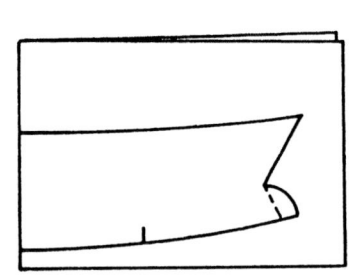

4. Transfer crossmarks to underside of paper. Cut out collar and open for completed pattern.

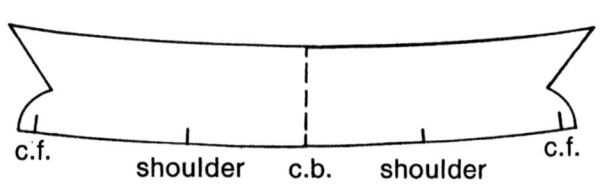

drafting sleeves

Sleeves are important assets to children's garments, and are also another area on garments that offer design possibilities—which is always exciting for the designer. Sleeves serve both a functional and decorative purpose. For example, spring and summer clothes may be sleeveless, fall and winter clothes need sleeves for warmth as well as for appearance.

There are two basic sleeve slopers, which can be used as they are *or* varied to suit a particular design. When planning the length and type of a sleeve, it is important to consider the entire design before deciding which sleeve design to use. If the dress design is rather simple, a sleeve in a contrasting fabric or color, or with trimming can become a focal point of the design. However, if the dress design already is exciting, *do not* detract from it with a busy sleeve. *Remember* you are dealing with a *small figure* that can handle only one or two points of interest. "When in doubt, leave it out," is a famous designer motto.

Sleeves may also be finished with piping, binding, ruffles, or band cuffs.

drafting basic long sleeves

1. Back of sleeve sloper is identified by two crossmarks on the cap; front of sleeve is identified by one crossmark on cap.

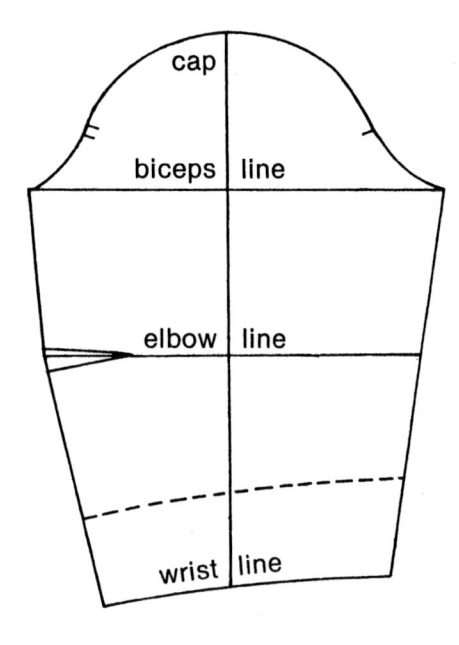

2. Avoid shortening sleeve or lengthening the basic sloper in the dart area. Work either above or below the elbow line.

3. If trimming is added to a long sleeve, shorten length at wristline equal to width of trimming. For example, for a 1" trimming shorten sleeve 1". *No* hem is needed on sleeve bottom if trimming is added. Plan for seam allowance on which to sew trimming.

4. When shortening or lengthening sleeve *below* elbow, measure up from wristline evenly to determine new wristline.

5. When shortening or lengthening sleeve *above* elbow, measure down from biceps line on underarm seam to determine new wristline. Draw straight line across sleeve. Underarm seams must be same length on front and back.

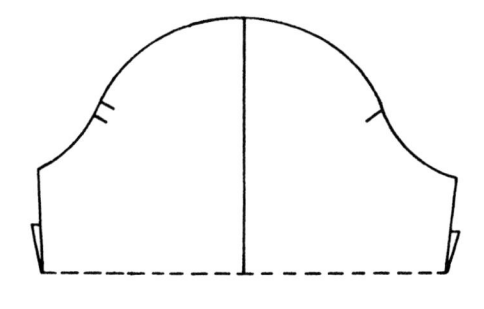

6. If trimming is not added, plan for a 1" to 1½" hem, depending on sleeve length and style.

7. Shape underarm seam below hem to underarm seam above hem by folding pattern back.

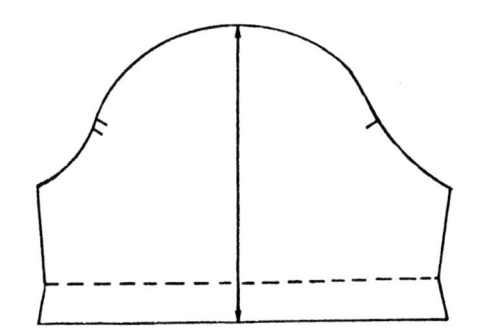

drafting short sleeves with shaped bottoms

1. Bottom of short sleeve can be shaped or curved. To be sure curve is identical on front and back of center line, fold sleeve in half on lengthwise grainline. Trace through with tracing wheel. True bottom of sleeve with French curve.

2. When bottom of sleeve is shaped, a facing is needed to finish edge (see DRAFTING FACINGS). Sleeve may also be cut with a lining (see SEWING SLEEVES).

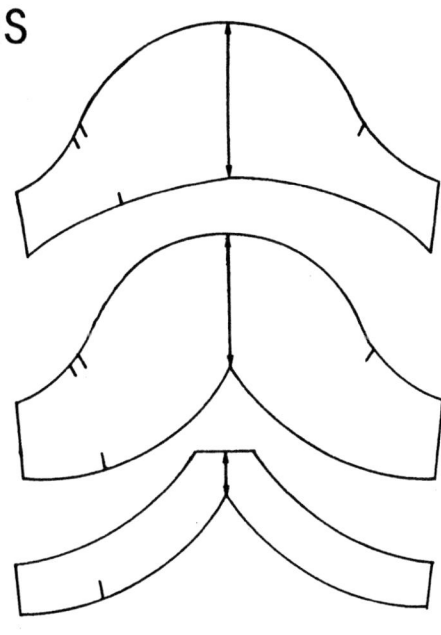

drafting puffed sleeves with band cuffs

1. Use *Puffed Sleeve Sloper* without any changes.

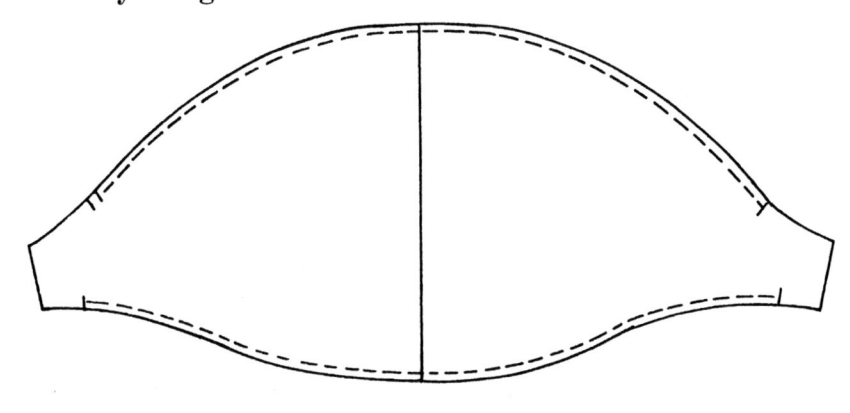

2. Measure upper arm of child and add ½" to measurement for ease for finished size of band.

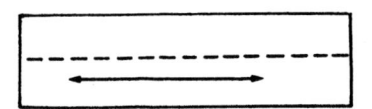

3. To determine width measurement for band, double desired finished width.

4. Draft pattern to measurements.

drafting puffed sleeves with self ruffles

1. Using *Puffed Sleeve Sloper*, measure down at center of sleeve at bottom edge about 1". Square a line out from center to underarm seam.

2. Draw underarm seam down to meet new line.

3. Measure up from bottom line desired amount for ruffle depth—1" to 1½". Elastic will be stretched across from underarm to underarm to form ruffle (see SEWING SLEEVES).

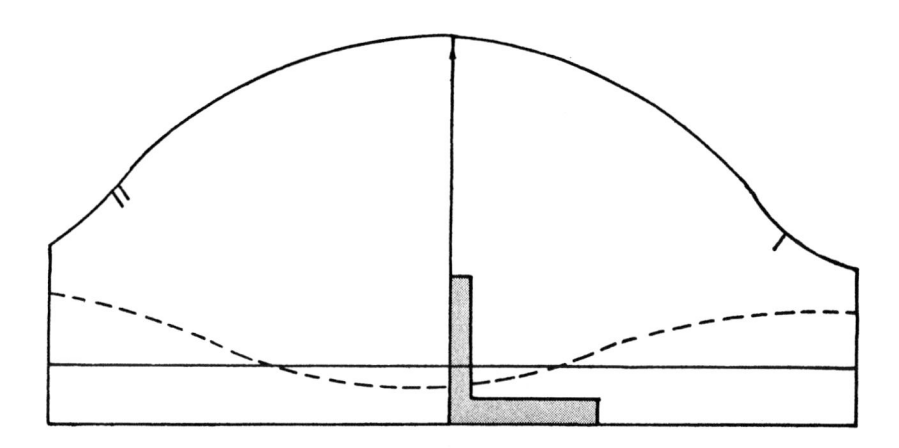

sportswear

Dressing in separates has come to be an important part of most adult wardrobes. The concept has extended into the children's wear market as well. It is a very practical idea, particularly for children who do not outgrow tops and bottoms as quickly as they outgrow one-piece garments.

Coordinated groups of garments planned as mix-and-match pieces are exciting to create and fun for children to wear. By coordinating colors, fabrics, trimmings, and design details many different outfits can be "put together." Fabric manufacturers feature color-coordinated fabrics to ensure that the colors and patterns in each group are perfectly matched.

Creating a coordinated group of garments can be achieved by simply making all the garments out of one or more matching fabrics. Another approach to a well-coordinated group is to trim each part with a trimming, appliqué, pocket or any motif that ties all the pieces together. There are infinite ways of working with separates. A reversible vest, for example, with a shirt and skirt makes a versatile group. Add a pair of pants and you have doubled the usefulness of all the pieces.

Skirts, blouses, shirts, vests, pants, and jumpers are all part of sportswear collections. Since pants, shirts, and vests are the same for boys and girls in these size ranges, the same slopers can be used for both.

drafting yokes

An important design feature used to vary the basic sloper is a yoke. The yoke falls primarily in the upper part of the garment and can assume many different shapes. Yokes can be planned for dresses, blouses, and jumpers.

Since the yoke cuts the sloper apart, the seam is an ideal place for additional trimming. Color and fabric combinations also work well with yokes. More than one fabric on a garment can be used. Most yokes on children's garments are made in the front and require very little fabric. Therefore, if you save scraps from your cuttings, you may often use fabrics from one garment to trim another.

1. Copy basic dress sloper onto another piece of paper for dress or jumper. Draft pattern for blouse if needed.

2. Plan yoke by holding paper sloper up to child and lightly sketching desired yoke (see DRAFTING NECKLINES) True line with French curve or ruler.

3. Crossmark about halfway between shoulder and center front. This crossmark will help you to assemble the garment accurately when sewing.

4. Separate yoke from body piece by carefully cutting yoke and dress section apart. Label each section and indicate grainlines.

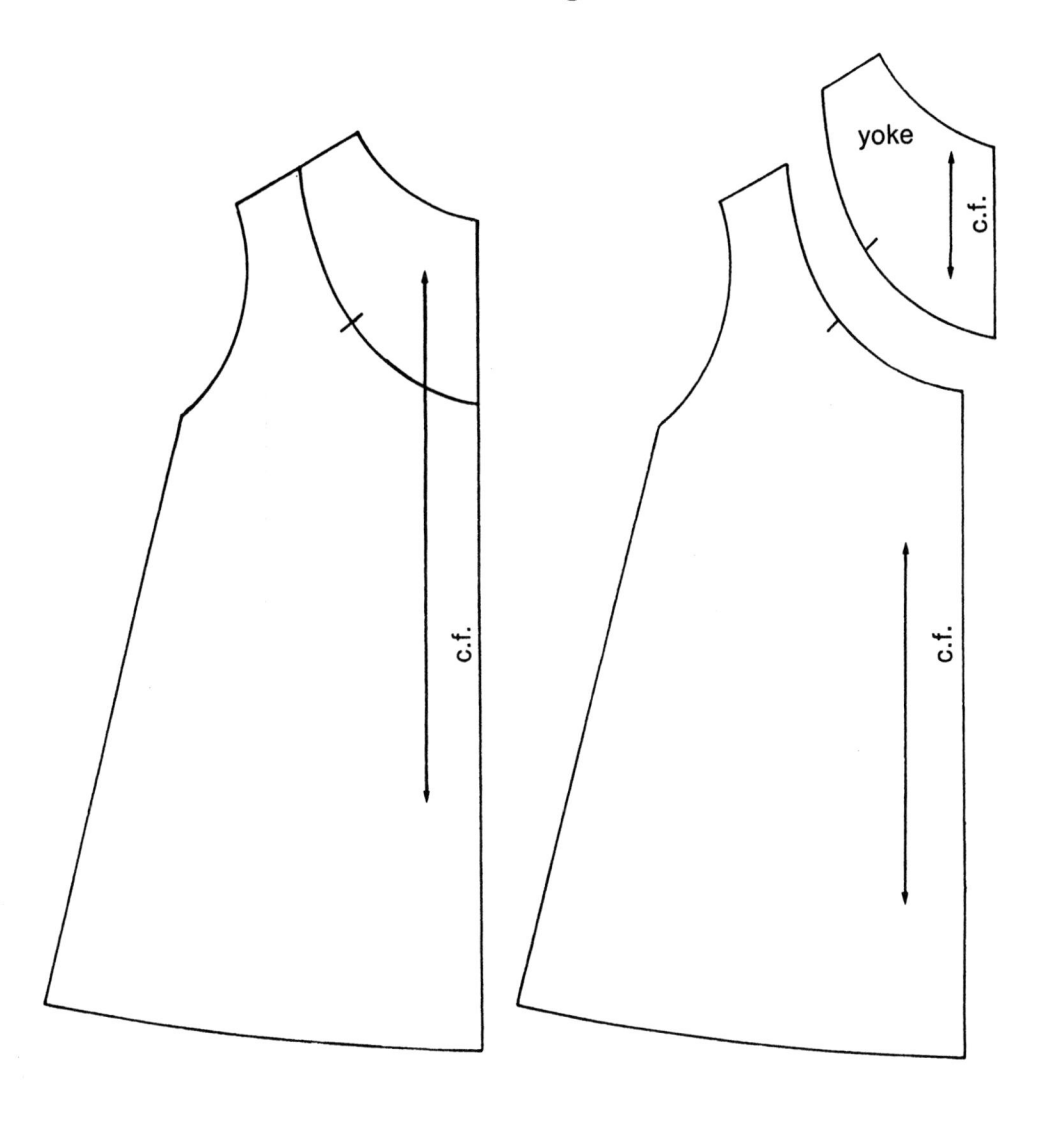

When styling the yoke, the design may call for the yoke to be completely separated from the bottom or skirt part of the pattern. This treatment opens up the possibility of adding fullness with gathers or pleats to the skirt. It also provides a seamline for adding trimmings between the two sections. This yoke with additional fullness, is described only for the straight yoke.

1. Place both front and back dress slopers on the child and determine the desired yokeline. (When slopers are on the figure the front and back yokelines should be balanced when viewed from the side.)

2. Follow instructions for trueing yokes discussed previously. Separate yoke from rest of sloper.

gathers

To determine the amount of fullness to add, consider the type of fabric used and the general silhouette of the garment you wish to make. Very thin fabrics will warrant more gathers than heavyweight fabrics.

1. Cut a sample piece of fabric and gather it to the amount of fullness that looks pleasing to you.

2. Measure the gathered piece and then release the gathers. The entire flat piece will then tell you how many times the finished size of fabric you will need to get the desired effect.

3. A general rule of thumb, however, is that two or three times to one gives a reasonable amount of fullness.

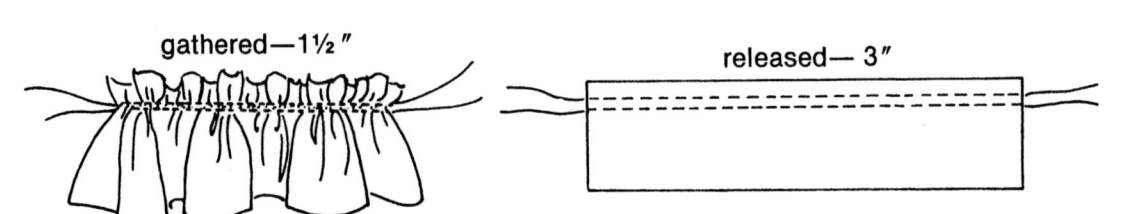

gathered—1½"

released— 3"

1. To determine the amount of gathers for the skirt/yoke design: add desired fullness to center front and center back of slopers. *Do not* change armhole shape. Plan gathers to end about 1″ to 1½″ from armhole edge and about 1″ from center back or center front seam, depending on placement of opening of garment. Crossmark to indicate end of gathers.

2. Complete pattern with markings as for yoke.

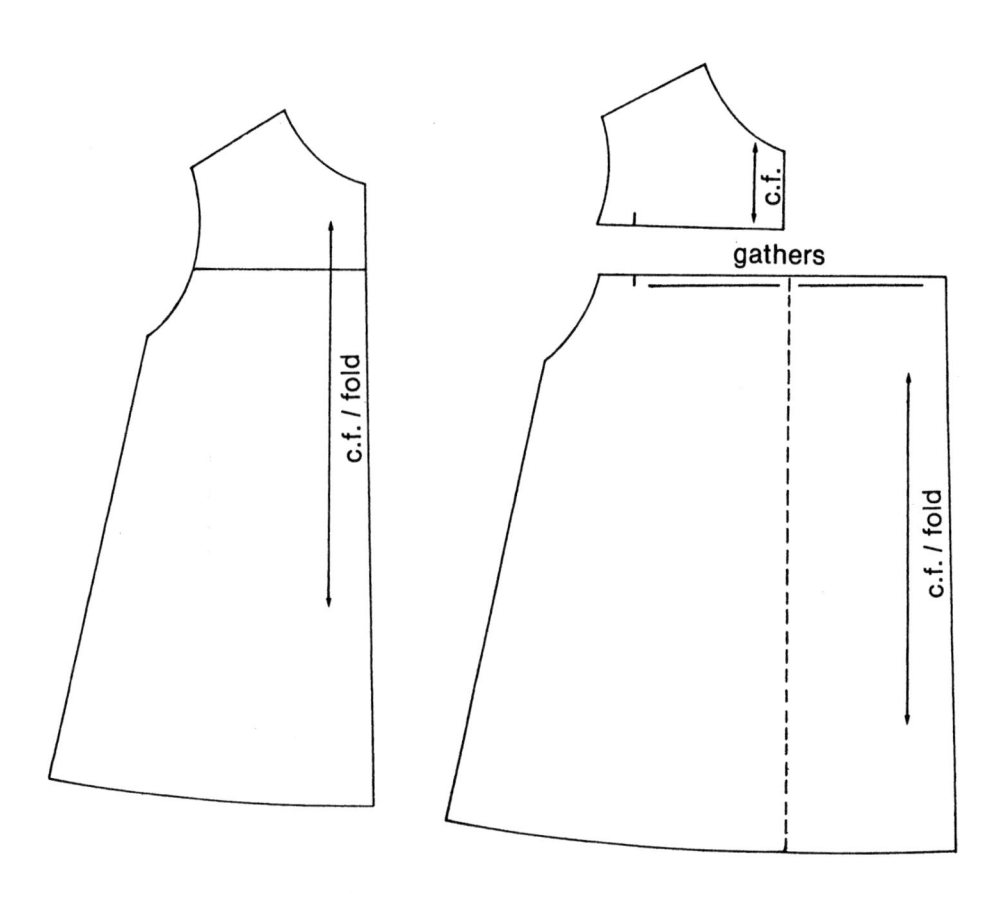

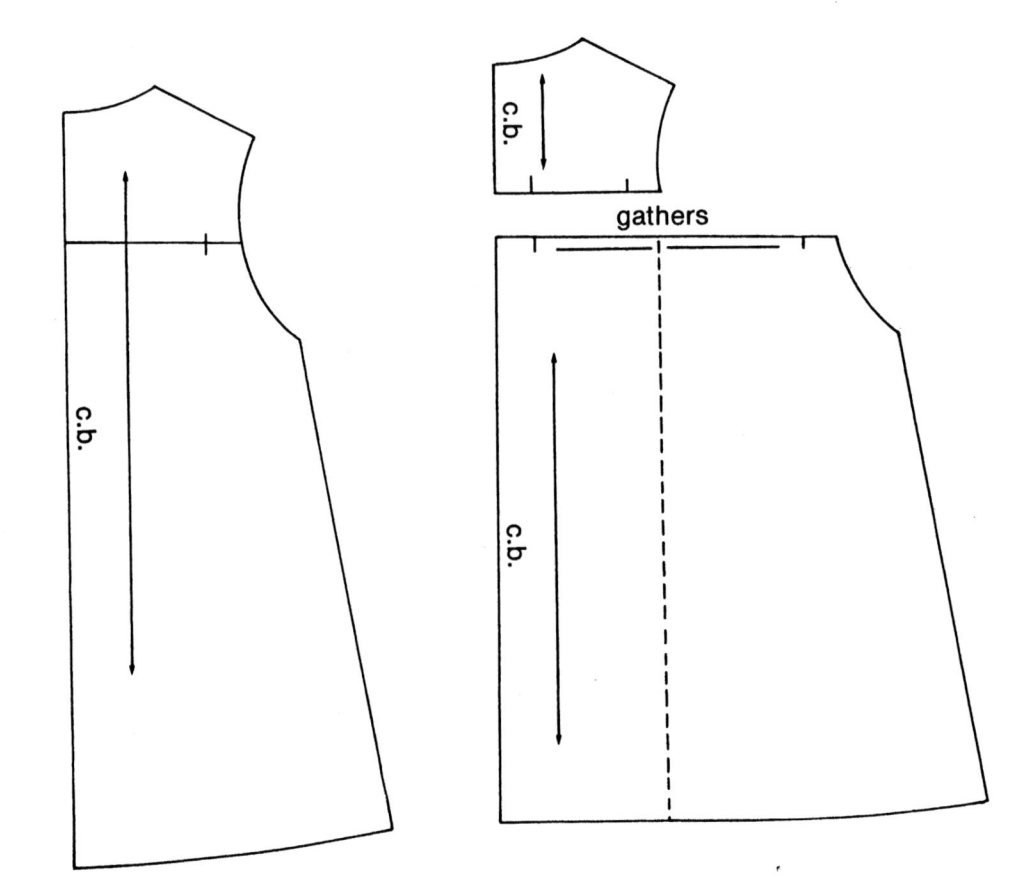

drafting blouses with straight yokes

Use the same method as for the dress or jumper. However, if fullness is to be controlled in a small area as in sketch, be sure to crossmark carefully.

1. Measure from center of pattern to beginning of gathers. Crossmark on yoke pattern (A to B).

2. Copy this crossmark onto bottom pattern matching centers (A to B).

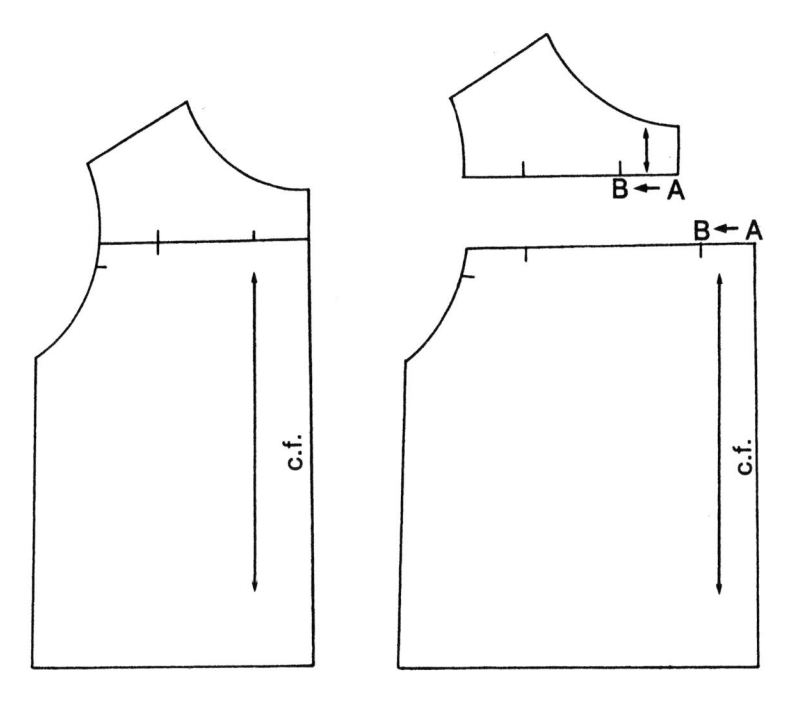

3. All the fabric between crossmarks will be gathered into yoke.

pleats

Pleats are used to add fullness and interest to a garment; they can be pressed or left unpressed. Some types of pleats are inverted, box, and side pleats. The depth of the pleats is part of the styling and should be determined as part of the design. Pleats usually are best planned on the lengthwise grainline.

inverted pleats

1. Start with a piece of paper large enough to accommodate the sloper, doubled, plus some extra for the pleats. Fold paper in half. Form pleat by folding the double thickness of paper to desired depth. Illustrated: 2″.

2. Place sloper on paper aligning center front of sloper with folded edge of paper. Trace sloper onto paper.

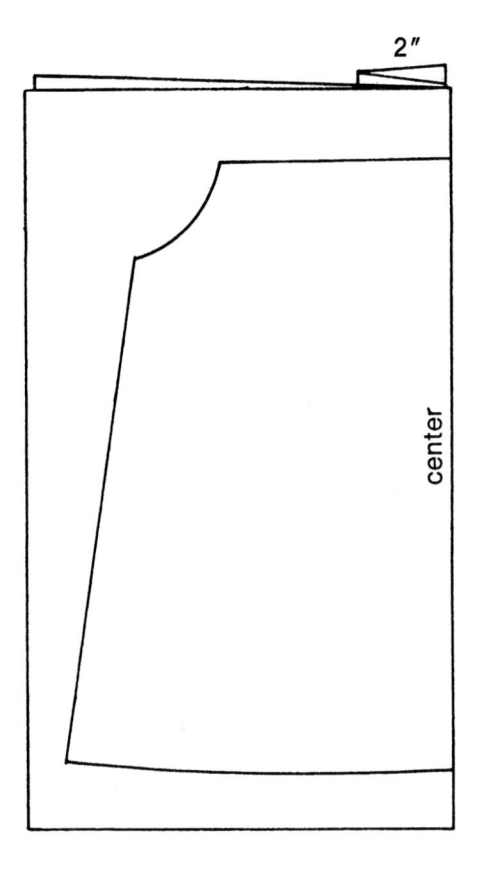

PATTERNMAKING/PLEATS

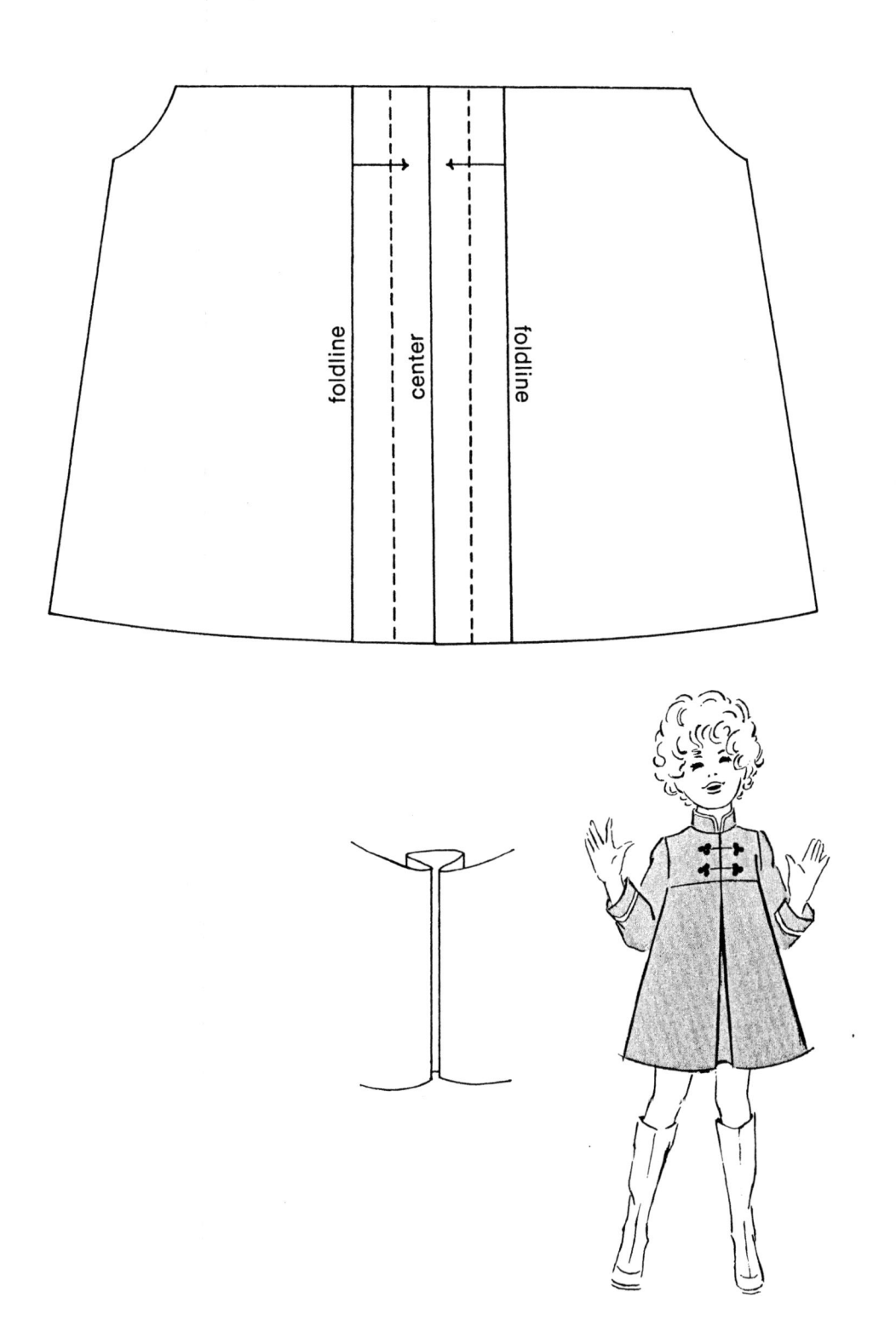

foldline
center
foldline

box pleats

A box pleat pattern can be developed following the same instructions as for INVERTED PLEATS, except that the direction of the folds is reversed.

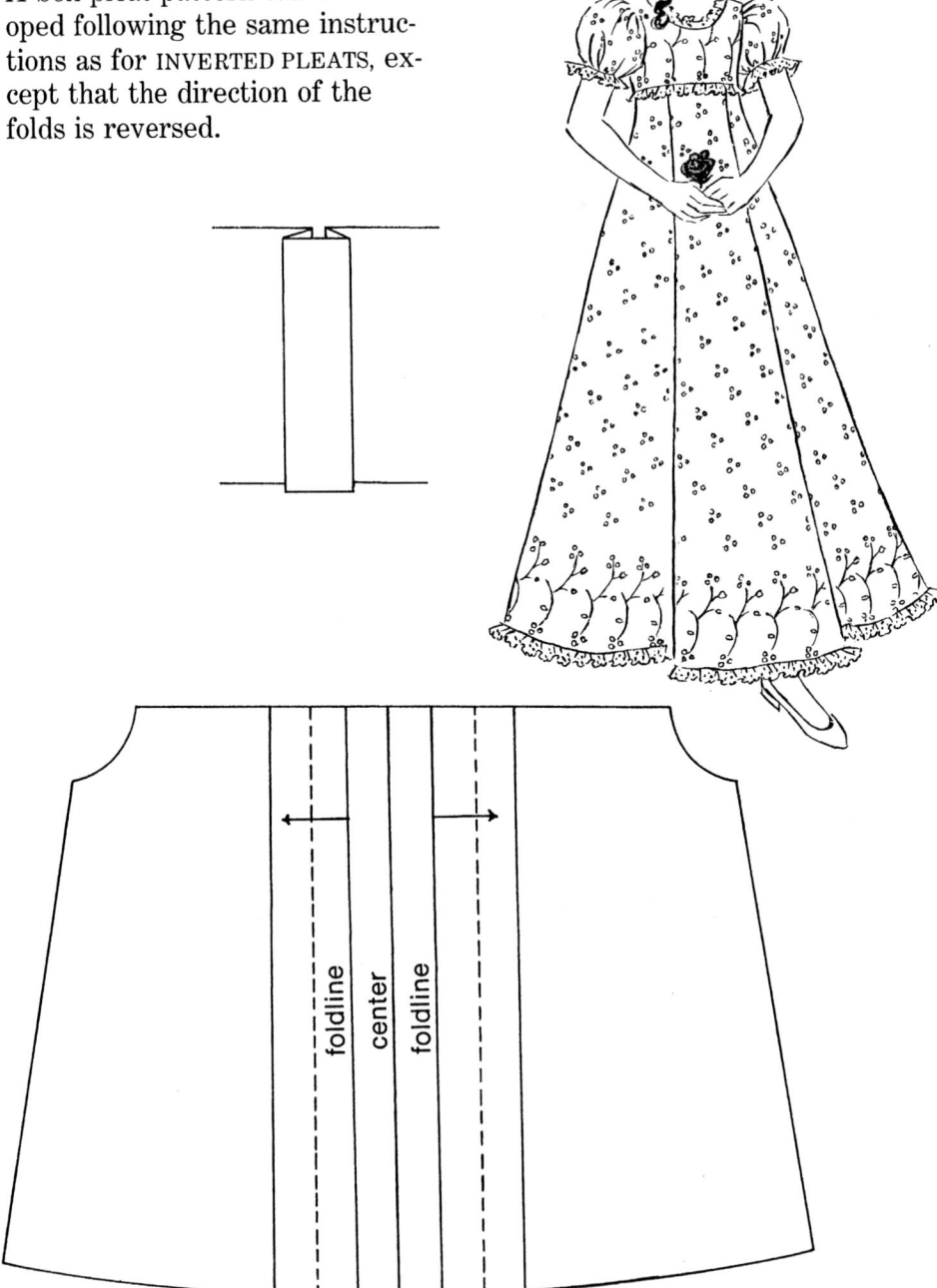

side pleats

Side pleat patterns are developed the same as for INVERTED PLEATS, except that the pleats face one direction. Side pleats should not extend into the armhole curve. Plan pleats to end 1″ to 1½″ from armhole edge.

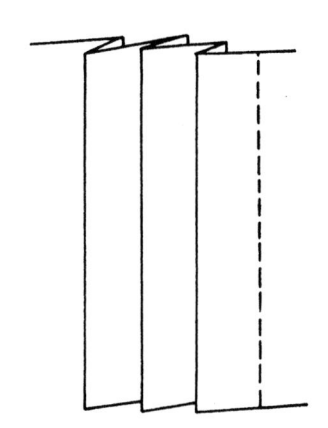

Pleats at the back of the garment are planned the same as for the front. Be sure to separate back into two parts to allow for an opening on the garment (see OPENINGS & CLOSINGS).

drafting blouses

To make a blouse pattern from the basic dress sloper, you will need the child's measurement from center back to waistline (see MEASUREMENT CHART). Add 5" to 7" to the measurement depending on the child's size.

1. Start with a piece of paper large enough to accommodate both the back and front dress slopers side by side.

2. Draw a straight line on the left-hand side of the paper about the length of the dress sloper at the center back. Label line A.

3. Square a line across the paper about halfway down line A. Label line B.

4. Square a line up and down from line B to correspond to A. Label line C.

5. Align back and front slopers on guidelines A, B, and C; center back on A; center front on C. Be sure the bottom of both armholes are on line B. Copy slopers.

6. Square a line down from line B at side seams on both slopers.

7. Measure down from center back neckline the desired finished length of blouse. Square across to side seam and continue the same line to center front. Both side seams must be the same length from armhole to hem.

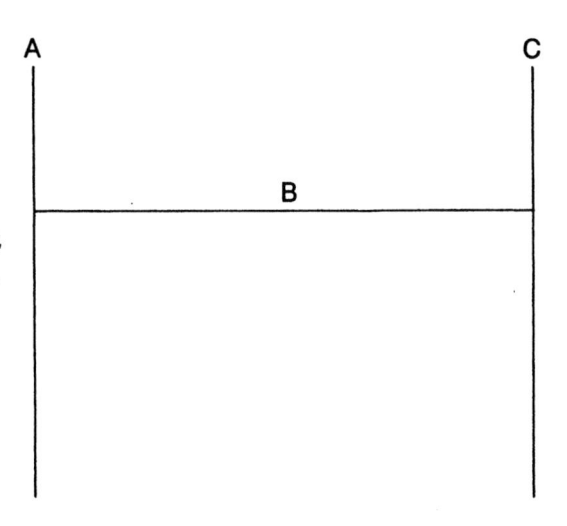

8. Complete patterns by planning for buttons and buttonholes at center front or center back (see OPENINGS & CLOSINGS).

9. All collar, sleeve, and yoke variations can be used in blouse designs.

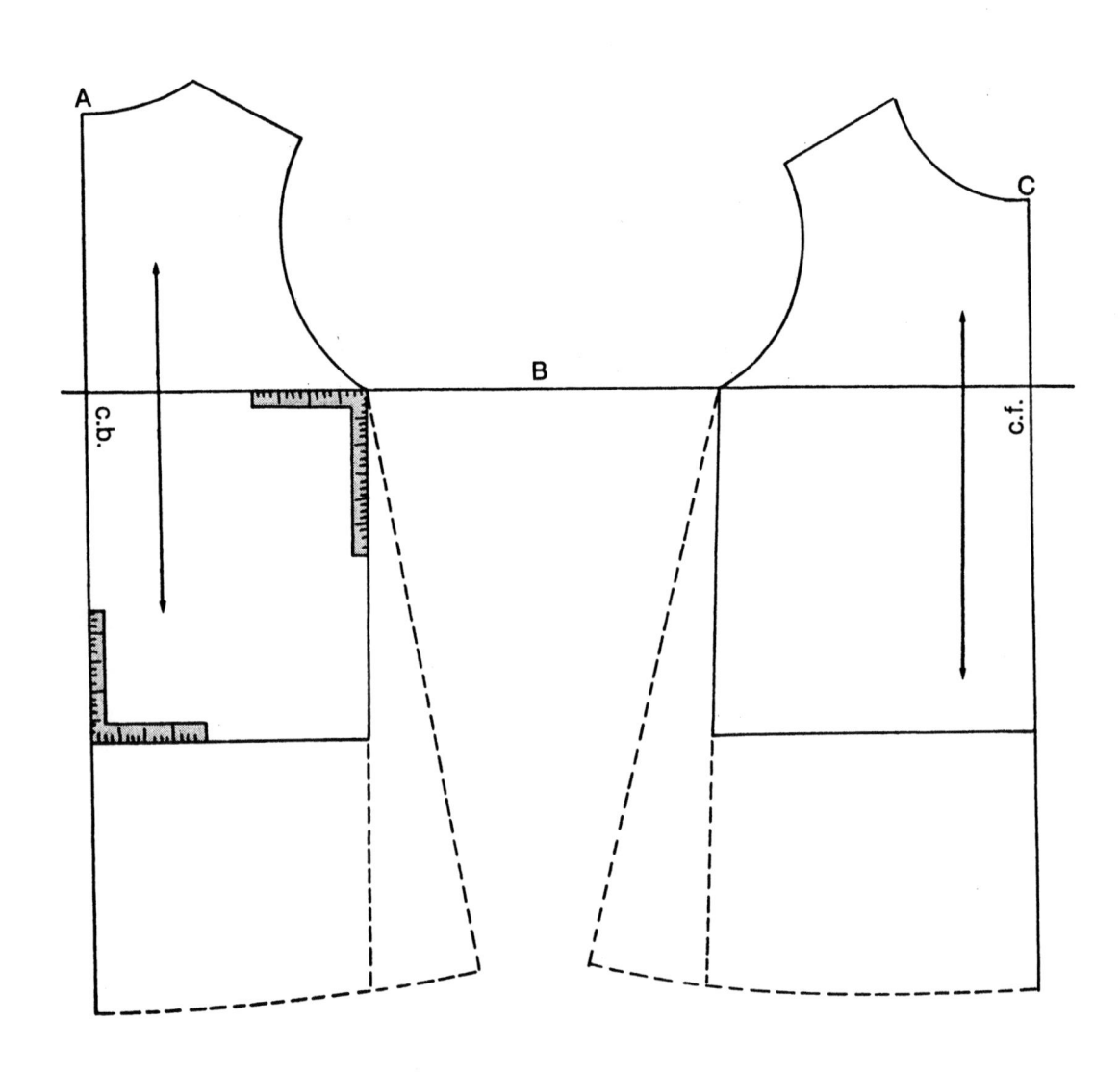

drafting shirts

To make a shirt pattern for boys or girls start with the blouse pattern.

1. Straighten armholes slightly and lower ¼" at side seam.

2. Add 2" for extension to center front for shirt front finish (seam allowance is included in this measurement). (See SEWING SHIRTS.)

3. Bottom can be shaped to give shirt-tail effect.

4. Use shirtwaist sleeve sloper and draft shirt collar to complete pattern.

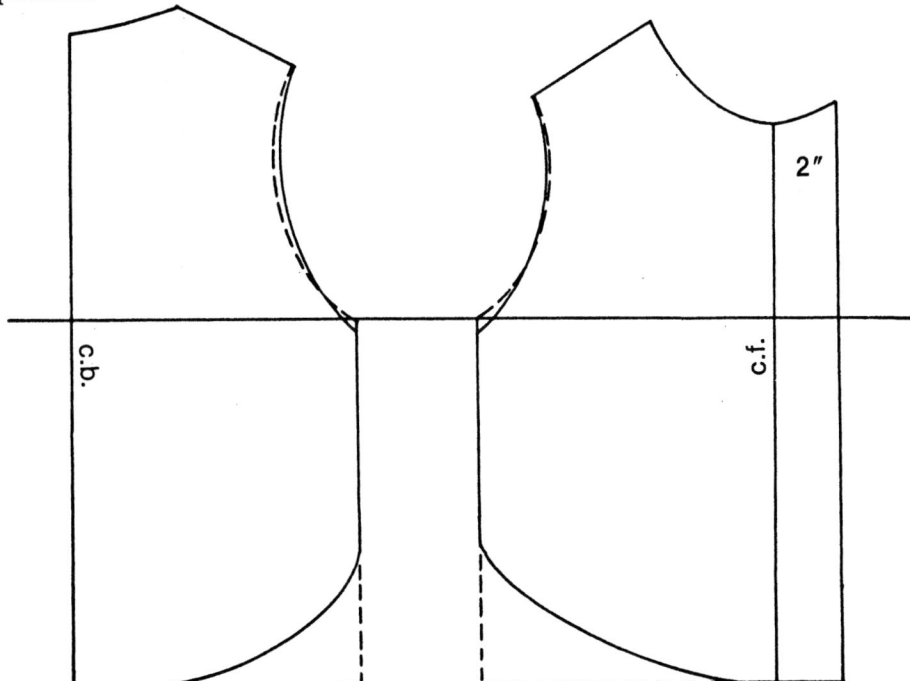

drafting vests

1. Follow Steps 1 and 2 for DRAFTING BLOUSES. Determine length of vest either by holding sloper up to child or model form or by using neckline to waistline measurement of size chart (see MEASUREMENT CHART). Vests normally fall in the waistline area at the back and can end in points below the waistline at the front.

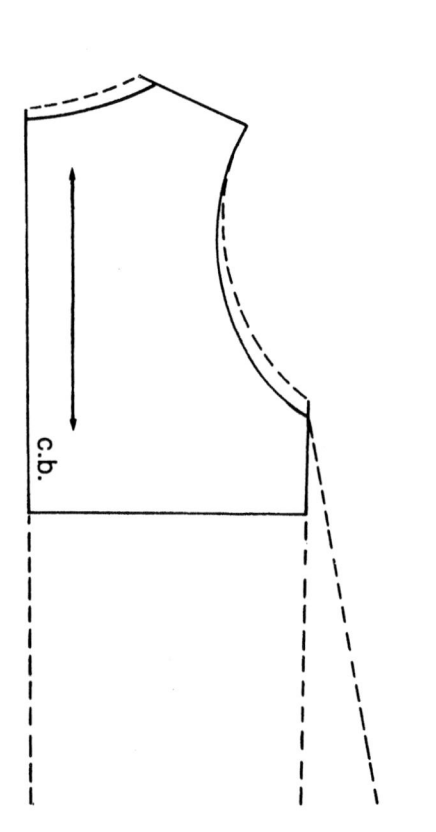

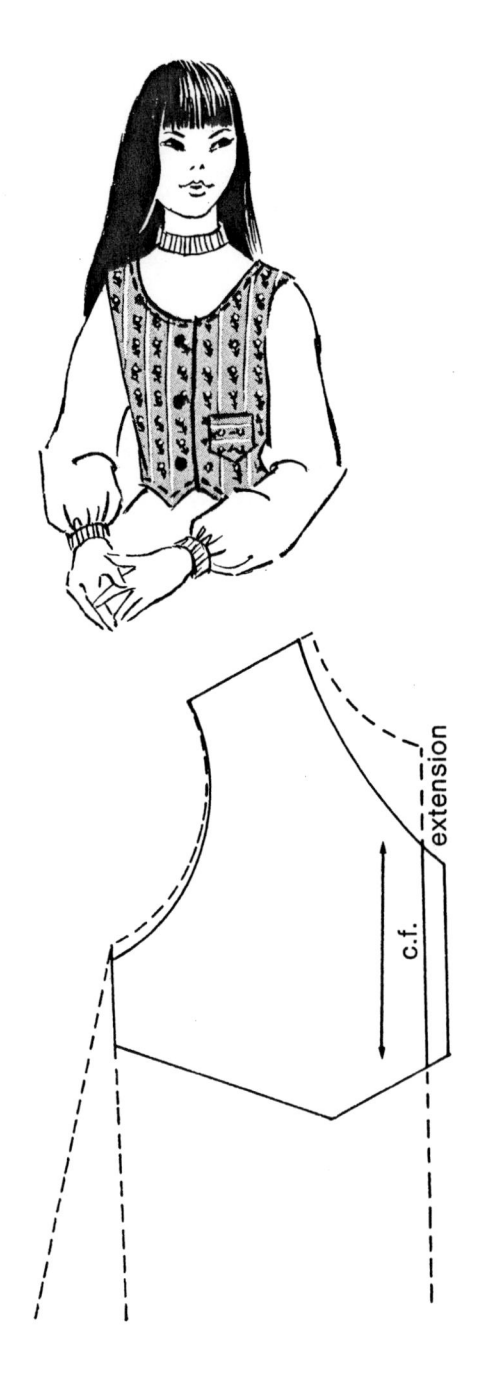

2. Square across from waistline/center back intersection to side seam. Match side seam length of front to back. Shape front into points. True line with French curve or ruler, depending on shape desired.

3. Shape neckline to a V-shape or as desired and true (see DRAFTING NECKLINES).

4. Lower armhole at side seam, ½".

5. See OPENINGS & CLOSINGS to complete pattern. If zipper is planned, use a separating zipper.

6. Armholes, front opening, and bottom of vest can be faced on larger sizes (size 8 and over). Smaller sizes should be lined, since facings are so small that they are difficult to handle. Cut lining from vest pattern.

drafting skirts

A very important part of any girl's wardrobe is a collection of skirts. Every sportswear line will contain a variety of skirts including the dirndl or gathered skirt, flare, wraparound, and variations on these styles.

Skirts can be designed with pleats, ruffled bottoms, pockets, surface design, such as appliqués, and many different kinds of trimmings. Little girls' skirt sizes (2, 4, 6) will probably need suspenders planned as part of the design to keep the skirts in place. WAISTBANDS and SUSPENDERS will be discussed on pages 89-92.

drafting dirndl or gathered skirts

The simplest skirt to make is the dirndl or gathered skirt.

1. Measure the child's waistline or use the MEASUREMENT CHART to determine waistline. Add ½" to measurement for ease.

2. Determine finished length and add 3" for hem allowance and 1" for seam allowance.

3. Determine the amount of fullness for skirt (see GATHERS). Two to three times the waistline measurement is usually adequate, depending on the type of fabric used.

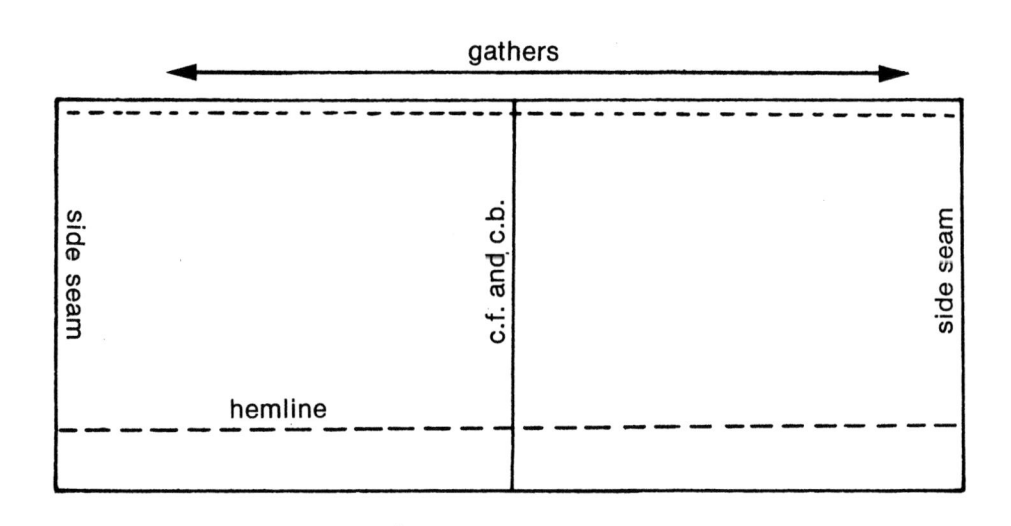

4. Plan for zipper or placket opening at side seam or center back. For side seam opening, front and back skirt patterns are exactly the same. Pattern will be a rectangle. For a center back opening, cut back skirt pattern in half. Add seam allowance.

5. For front button opening, cut front skirt pattern. Plan sufficient fabric for extension and fold-back facing. Crossmark about ½" from center front line for gathers. Gathers should not extend into extension or facing.

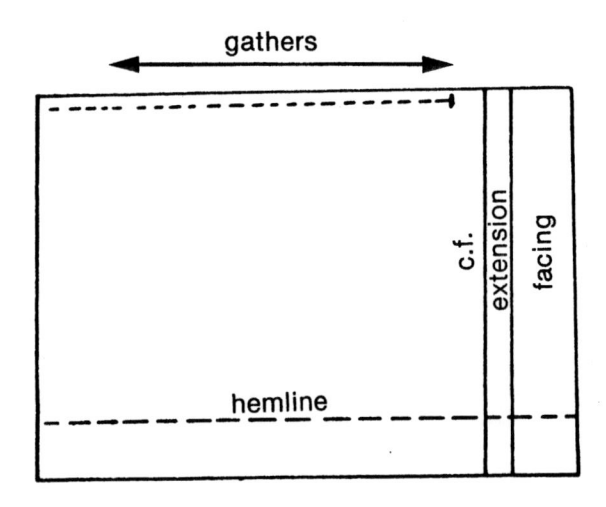

drafting flare skirts

1. Use skirt sloper without changes or with some variation. Use the same sloper for front and back skirt patterns.

2. Pleats can be added to center front and/or center back (see PLEATS).

3. Pockets can also be added.

4. When a plaid fabric is used, skirt can be cut on the bias.

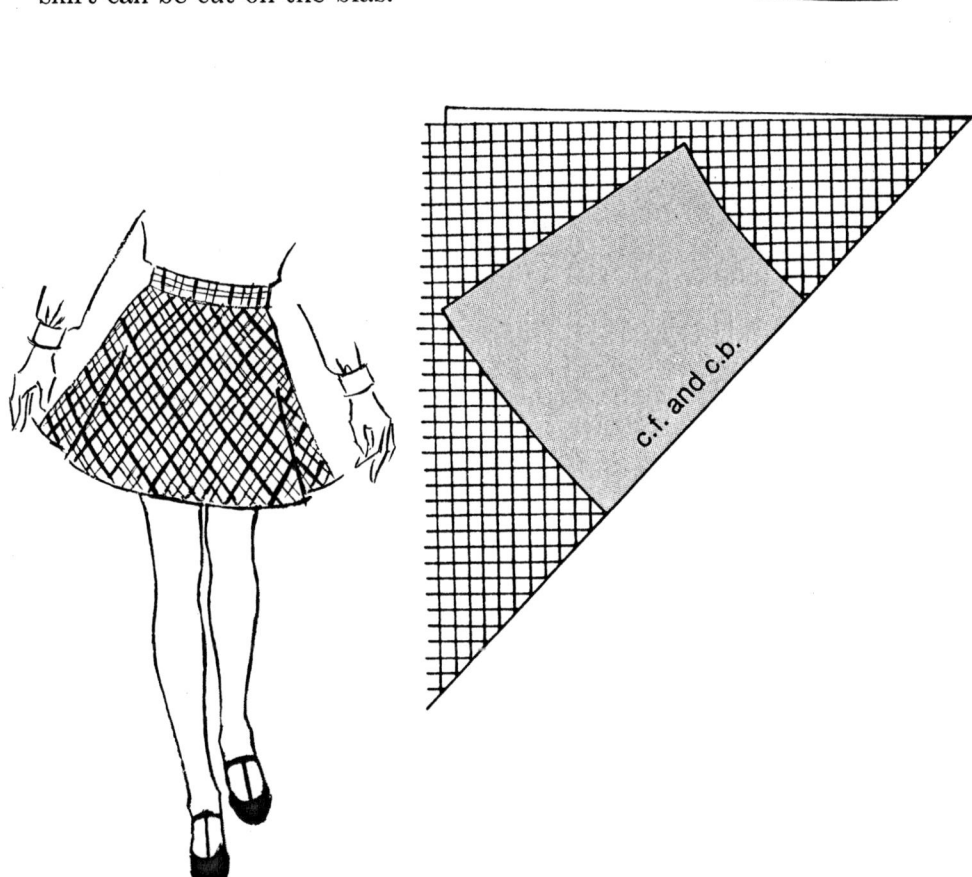

5. Skirt may be cut on the straight of the fabric. If plaid fabric is used, match plaid at side seam (see LAYING OUT & CUTTING PATTERNS IN FABRIC).

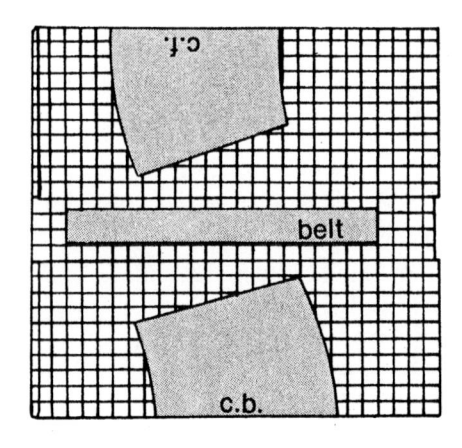

drafting wraparound skirts

1. Start with a piece of paper large enough to accommodate the entire front skirt pattern. Fold paper in half and align center front of skirt sloper to fold. Trace skirt sloper.

2. With tracing wheel, trace skirt sloper to other side of paper. Open paper and determine placement of extension. Be sure there is sufficient fabric to lap over and stay closed (2" to 4" depending on size of garment).

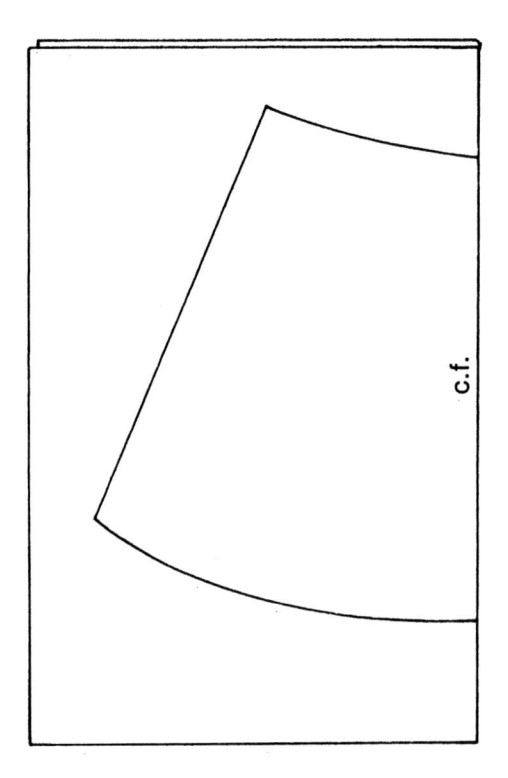

3. Cut out identical pattern for both sides of front skirt.

4. Use basic skirt sloper for back of skirt.

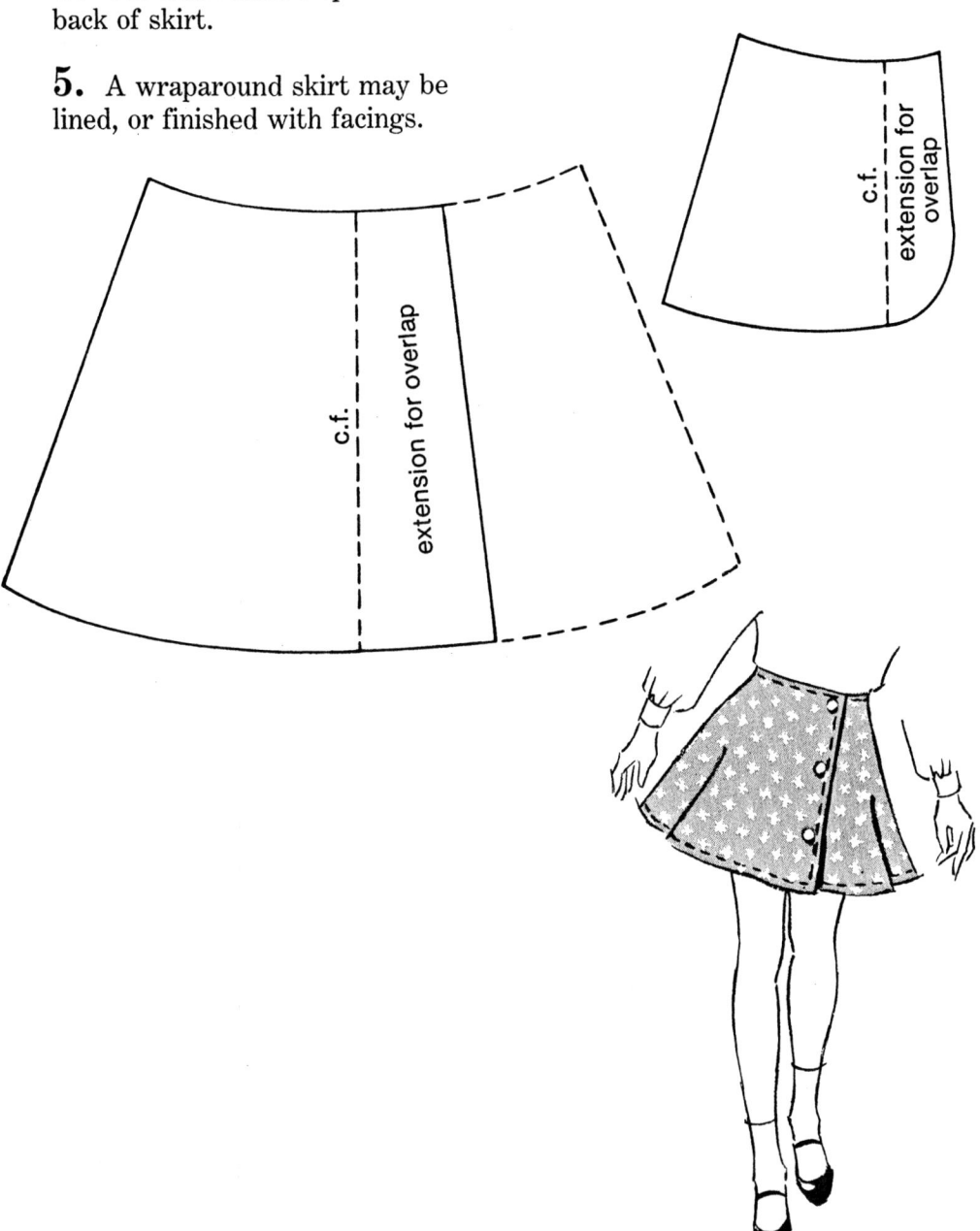

5. A wraparound skirt may be lined, or finished with facings.

drafting jumpers

A jumper is a one-piece sleeveless garment, generally worn over a blouse or sweater. A jumper is a great way to vary a child's wardrobe. It has the advantages of a skirt, because it can be worn with different tops, and the neatness of a dress, because it does not come apart at the waistline the way separates do.

The jumper pattern is made from the *basic dress sloper*. All the pattern drafting techniques for the dress can be applied to the jumper.

1. Using the dress sloper, lower the armhole ½" and extend the side seam ¼" (as illustrated). These adjustments allow for comfort when the jumper is worn over a blouse or sweater.

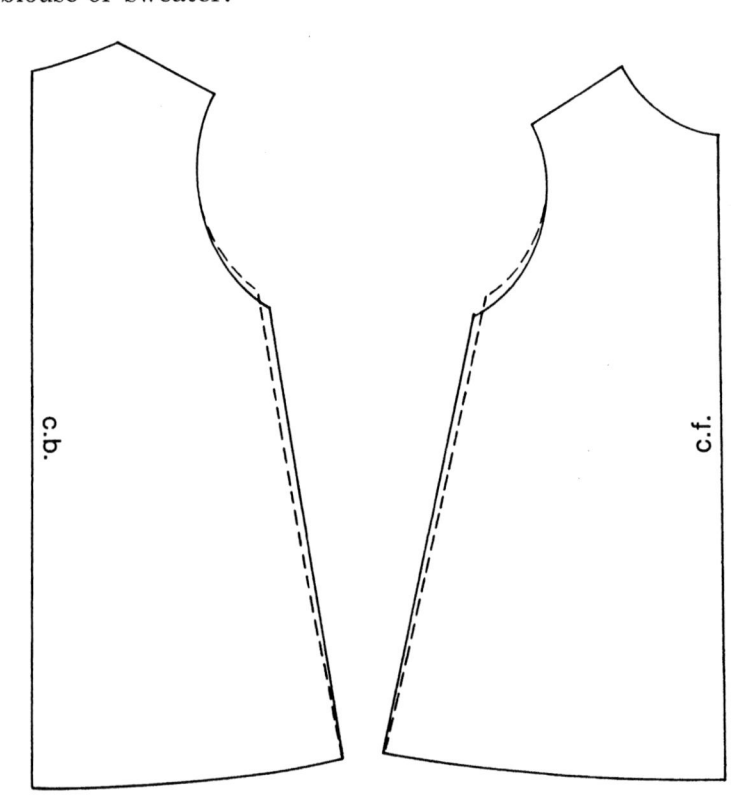

2. Use any neckline variation. If a high round neckline is planned, lower neckline evenly all around ½".

3. Finish the armhole and neckline of the jumper with facings (see FACINGS).

4. Allow for zipper or button and buttonhole closings at center front or center back. Jumpers can also be opened at the shoulders eliminating the need for back or front openings as discussed below.

drafting jumpers with scoop necklines & front pleats

1. Draft jumper pattern from basic dress sloper.

2. See DRAFTING NECKLINES for instructions on neckline shape.

3. See INVERTED PLEATS for instructions on folding paper.

4. Copy jumper pattern with new neckline onto paper marked and folded for pleat.

5. Cut out pattern. Mark center front foldline and pleat lines. Indicate with a crossmark how far down to stitch pleat.

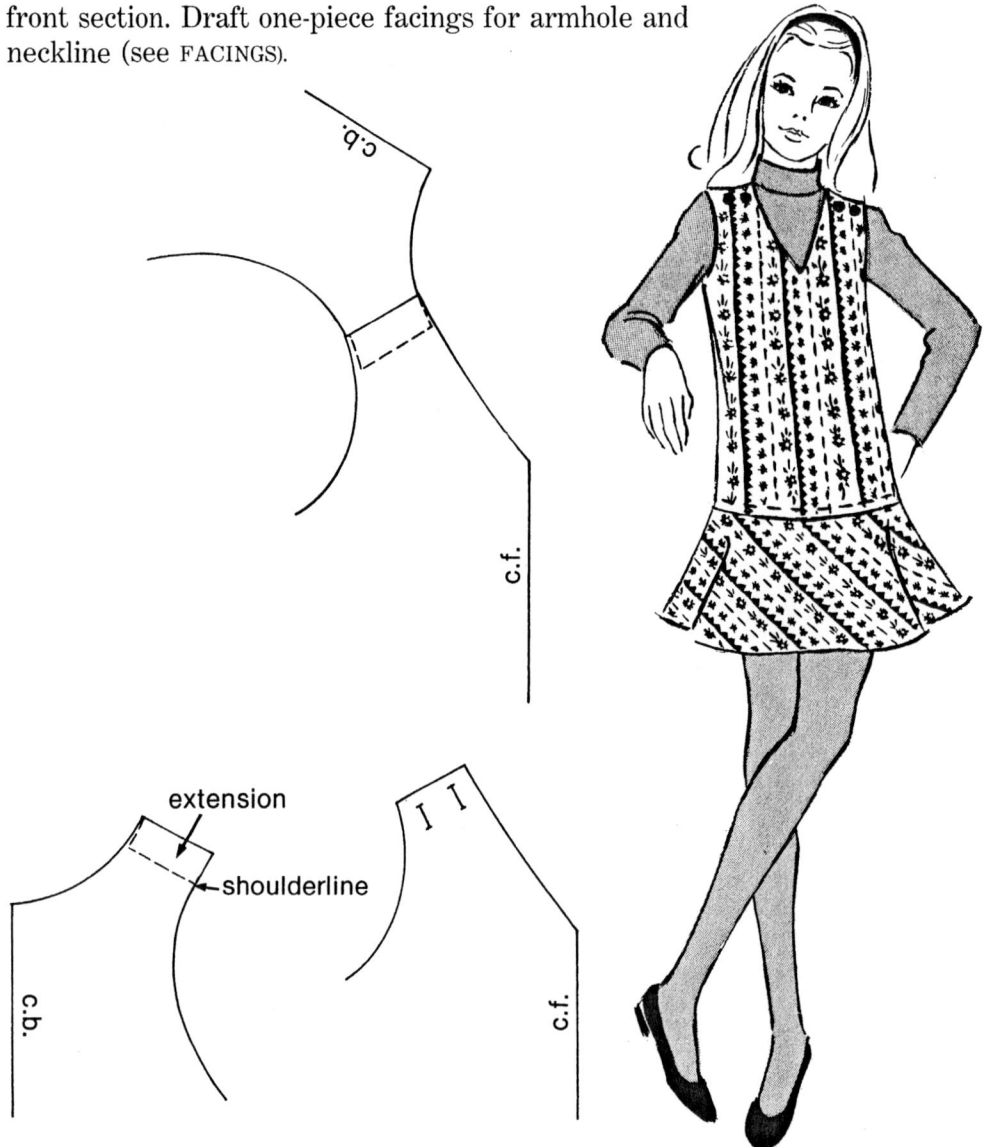

drafting jumpers with shoulder openings

To open shoulders on jumper for buttons and buttonholes, extend back shoulder towards front, following front shape for about 1". *Do not* change front shoulder. Place front and back shoulder seams together to determine placement of buttons and buttonholes. Mark buttonholes on front section. Draft one-piece facings for armhole and neckline (see FACINGS).

drafting jumpers with lowered waistlines

1. Draft jumper pattern from basic dress sloper. Determine position of lowered waistline by holding pattern up to child. Lightly sketch line for desired lowered waistline.

2. Measure up evenly from bottom of pattern to determine new lowered waistline and true. Repeat for back.

3. Cut pattern apart.

4. Draft neckline to a V-shape (or to any desired neckline, see DRAFTING NECKLINES).

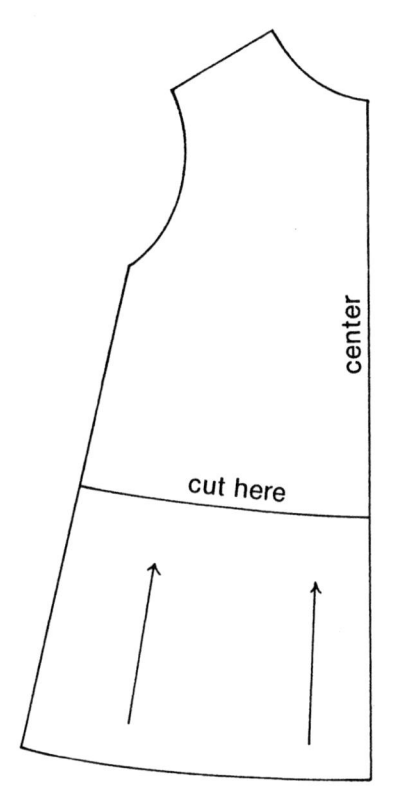

5. Follow instructions for DRAFTING BOX PLEATS. Place lower section of pattern on paper folded for pleat. Copy this section.

6. Repeat for back pattern.

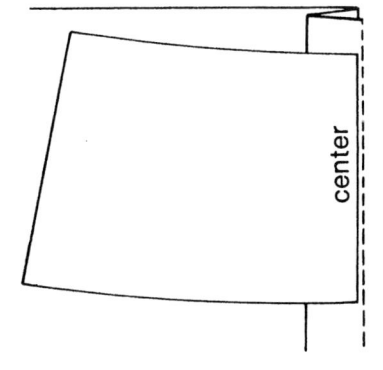

drafting pants

An indispensable item in any child's wardrobe, boy or girl, is pants. Children need pants and/or shorts in a variety of lengths for school, play, and dress-up.

The basic pants sloper can be used for boys or girls with adjustment from full-length pants to shorts, drafted to your own specifications.

When planning full-length pants, check the side seam length of the child from waistline to ankle and adjust the sloper if necessary. Shorten or lengthen at the bottom of the pants.

1. Shorts patterns can be made from the basic pants sloper by cutting the sloper at the dotted line.

2. To make patterns for longer shorts which fall just above-the-knee, and knicker-length pants, which fall below-the-knee, measure child or model form from waistline to desired finished length at the side seam.

3. Measure up evenly from the bottom edge of the sloper to determine cutting line on front and back.

drafting boxer pants

Boxer pants are basic pants with a boxer waistline (elastic all around). These pants do not have a fly-front opening and are suitable for girls or very small boys (size 2).

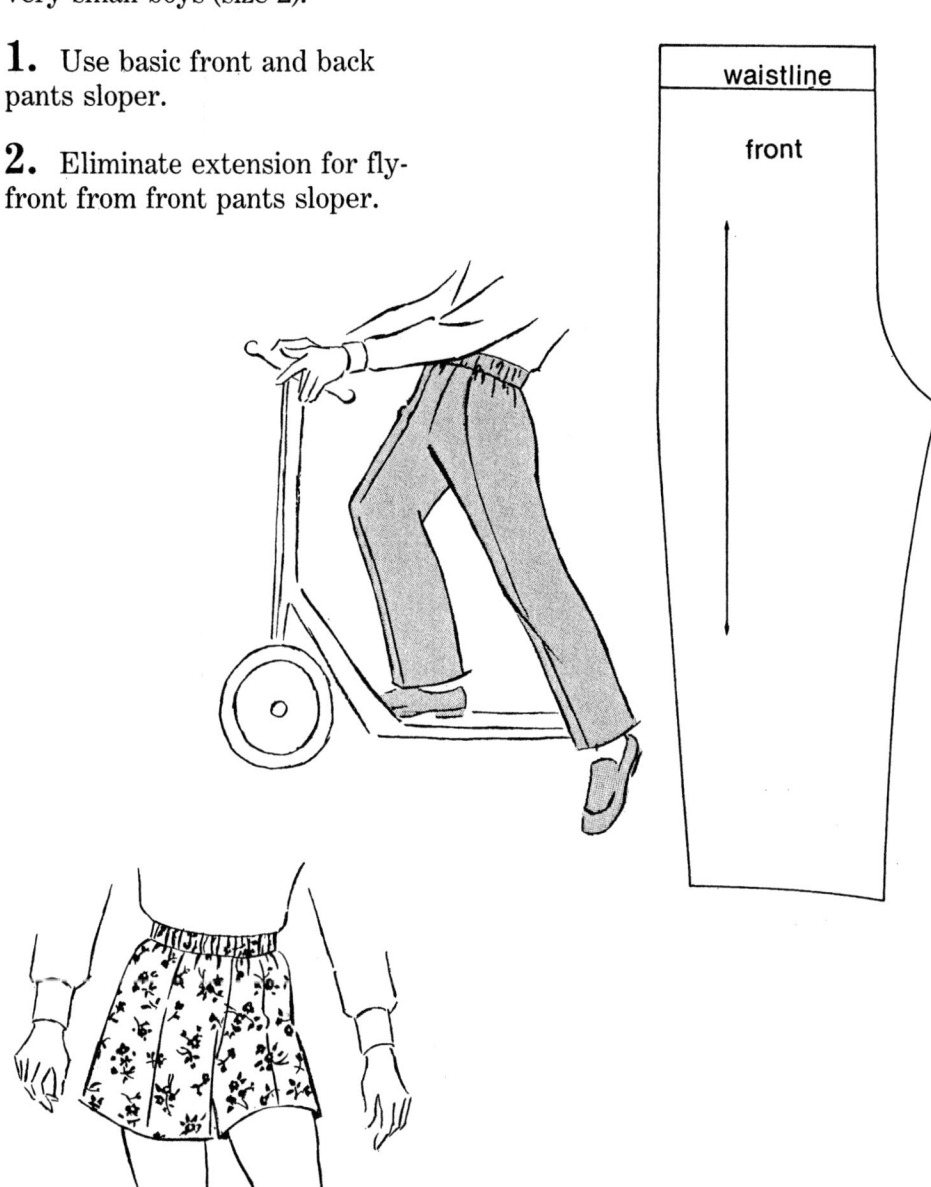

1. Use basic front and back pants sloper.

2. Eliminate extension for fly-front from front pants sloper.

drafting fly-front pants

The pants illustrated have a fly-front opening and a separate waistband in front only. They are elasticized in the back.

1. Use basic front and back pants sloper.

2. Eliminate casing from front pants sloper, *but* remember to add seam allowance for sewing on waistband.

3. Plan waistband to finish the same width as the casing. Measure from side seam to center front plus extension for front closing.

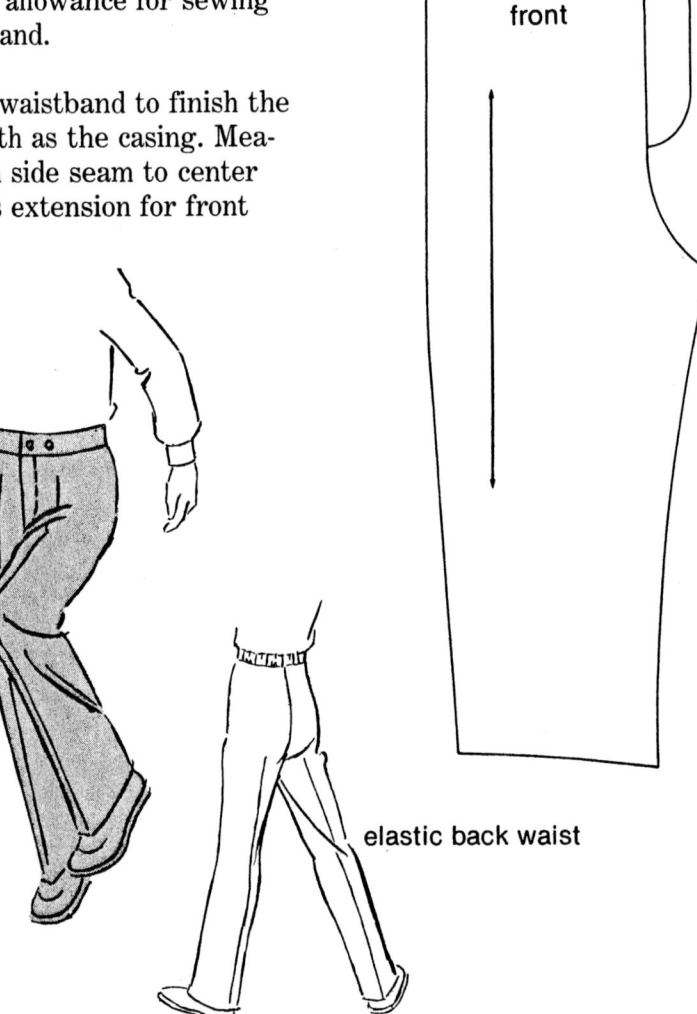

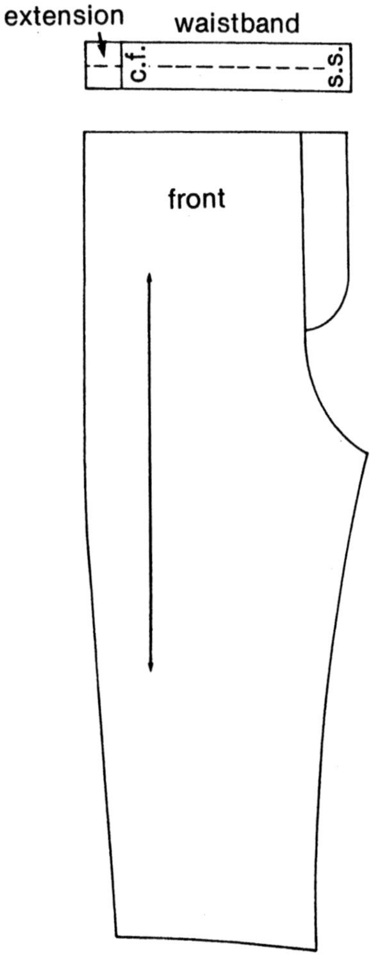

elastic back waist

drafting fly-front pants with trouser pockets

1. Use basic front and back pants sloper plus drafted waistband.

2. Determine placement of pocket line.

3. Draw in pocket shape with outside finished line and pocket opening.

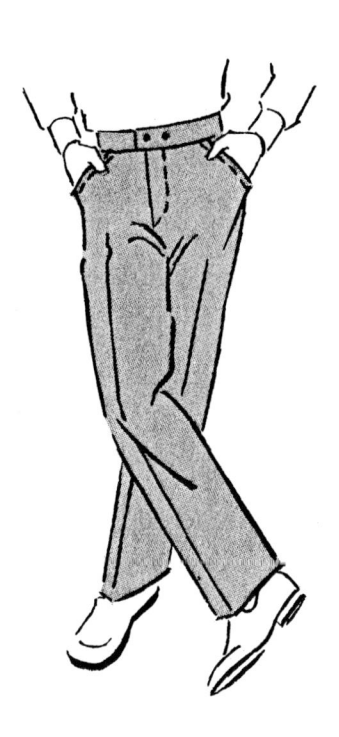

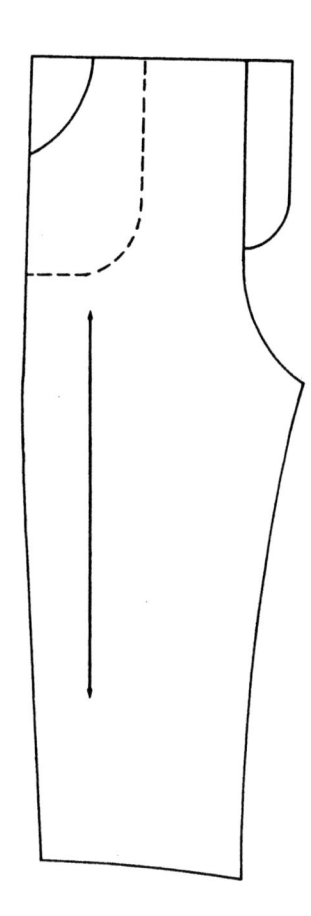

4. Copy shaded area onto another sheet of paper. This becomes the back of the pocket and the upper part of the pants.

5. Copy lower pocket. This becomes pocket facing.

6. Cut pants on pocket line.

7. Pattern is made up of three separate sections (as illustrated).

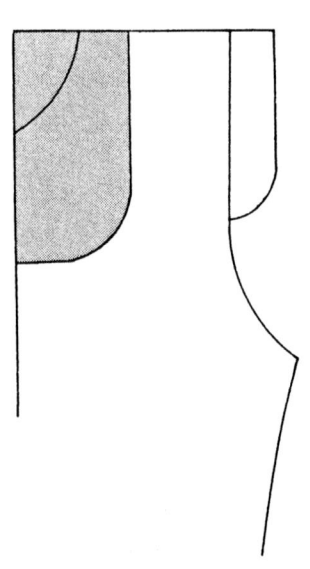

This method for drafting pockets can be applied to any style of pants or skirts.

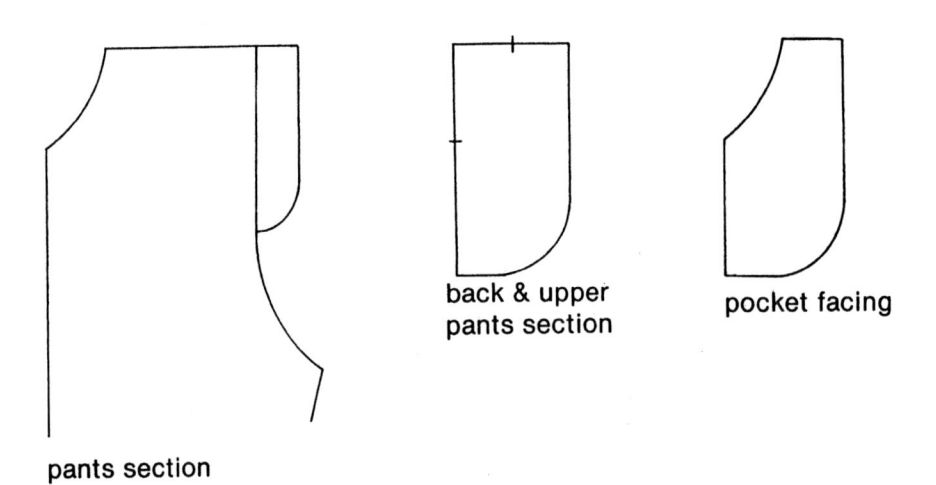

pants section

back & upper pants section

pocket facing

drafting waistbands for skirts or pants

1. To determine width of waistband, measure waistline of skirt or pants with a tapemeasure and add ½" for ease. Determine width of waistband, and double. Add 1" for seam allowance. Children's waistbands are usually ¾" to 1¼" wide, with 1" being the most popular width.

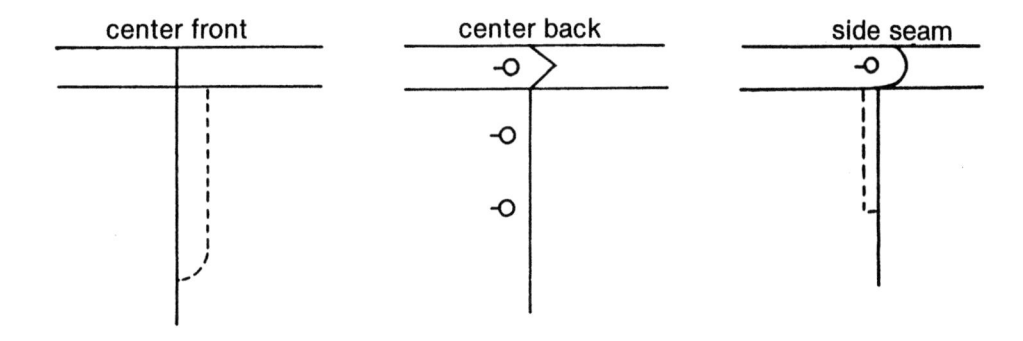

center front

center back

side seam

c.f.   s.s.   c.b.   s.s.   c.f.

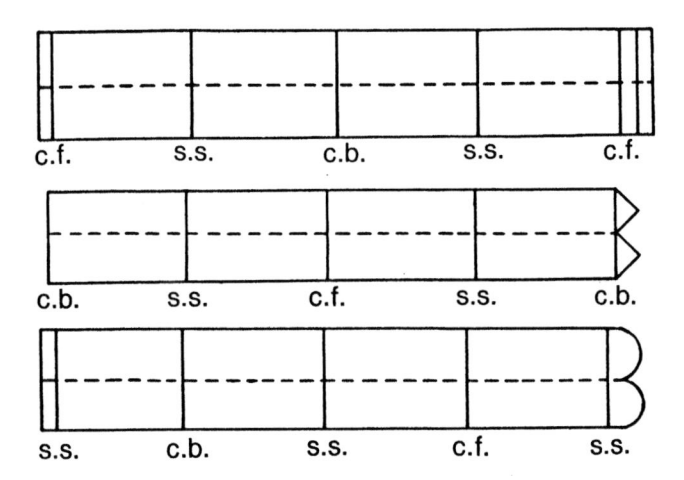

c.b.   s.s.   c.f.   s.s.   c.b.

s.s.   c.b.   s.s.   c.f.   s.s.

2. Draw the waistband on paper to the correct measurements, squaring the corners. Divide the waistline measurement into quarters, and mark on waistband corresponding to placement of opening on skirt or pants. For example, for a center back opening, the ends of the waistband will meet at center back. If skirt has side seam opening, ends of waistband will meet at side seam.

drafting suspenders for skirts or pants

1. Measure child or model form from front waistline area to back waistline area over the shoulder. Crossover-on-the-back suspenders stay up on the child better than straight-over-the-shoulder suspenders. Add 3" to 4" for adjustment.

2. Plan width of suspenders to correspond to width of skirt waistband. A 1" wide skirt waistband will require 1" wide suspenders.

3. Draft suspenders as for waistband. Indicate lengthwise grain on suspenders.

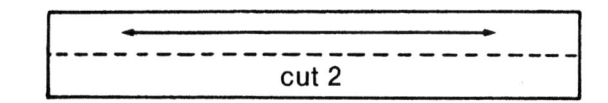

cut 2

4. Plan for buttonholes to hold suspenders on waistband (or bib); sew buttons to suspenders for easy adjustment as child grows.

drafting suspenders with a bib

1. Plan for bib by measuring width and length on child or model form. Draft pattern to desired shape.

2. Measure for suspender length from top of bib.

cut 2

c.f. / fold

UNIT FOUR
SEWING CHILDREN'S CLOTHING

The sewing techniques discussed in this text, are basic procedures used in the construction of children's garments. They are not geared to a *specific* garment. You will note that I have not discussed sewing blouses or vests. The procedures for sewing these types of garments are the same as for dresses and facings.

You are creating original designs. This means that you will have to *adapt* the general construction techniques to your specific needs. Use the instructions as a guide. Plan the steps and methods you are going to use before you begin sewing. You may at times, have to combine more than one method because of a design feature. As in any area of creativity you will, at times, break new ground. Being a designer means not only creating the original idea, but following through to the finished product. The follow-through in sewing is sometimes as challenging as the original design.

basic sewing instructions

After the pattern pieces are cut out in the desired fabric and marked, you are ready to assemble the garment.

- For All Garments
    1. Complete all surface decoration of the garment such as the embroidered yoke or pockets, appliqué, or trimming.
    2. Prepare all small pieces such as collars, sleeves, pockets, and belts.

- For Dresses, Blouses & Jumpers
    3. Sew front and back shoulder seams together.
    4. Complete neckline with collar, facings, or bindings.
    5. Sew separate skirt to bodice or yoke at front waist and back waist. *Do not* sew side seams.
    6. Finish seam for zipper. Fold-back facing for buttons.
    7. Sew sleeves into open armhole.
    8. Sew side seams from sleeve edge to hem edge.
    9. Finish hem.

pressing

A vital part of sewing in order to achieve a really professional look for garments is *pressing*. The difference between, "You made it yourself? I can tell," and "You made it yourself, I don't believe it," is very often in the pressing.

Press each garment section as it is completed and before it is attached to the next section. Press all seams immediately after stitching them. *No* garment can be successfully pressed *after* it is completely assembled.

seams & seam finishes

Every garment you construct will have seams and seam allowances—seams are the stitches that hold the garment together. If you have added the seam allowance to the pattern and are a beginning sewer, you may want to trace the sewing lines from the paper pattern onto the fabric. This is done with a tracing wheel and carbon tracing paper specially prepared for sewing.*

If you have used the shorter method of adding ½" seam allowance directly onto the fabric and have cut the fabric very accurately, you can stitch seamlines by measuring in from the cut edge ½" as you sew. It is very important that you sew seam allowances exactly. If you have allowed ½" and proceed to stitch at ¼" for example, the finished garment will be too big. Even though ¼" seems very minimal, remember it involves two parts of the garment which will equal ½" and a significant amount on a small garment.

The type of seam finish used for each garment will depend on the fabric and the type of garment being constructed.

---

*Use white or pale yellow colored carbon tracing paper. Colored paper such as red or blue can leave stains which are difficult to remove.

Plain seams are not as strong as flat-felled or French seams, but not all areas of the garment are under stress. Plain seams are easier to sew on curved edges as well as on bulky or excessively stiff fabric. When in doubt it usually pays to take the time to test various seam finishes on a scrap of fabric.

Flat-felled seams are stitched with two rows of stitches and provide the double advantage of being extra strong and completely encasing the raw edge of the seam. These seams are made on a double-needle machine in the garment industry and are cost effective.

The *French seam* is a more costly finish because there is no machine to sew it in one operation as with the flat-felled or double-needle machine stitch. It is a good finish for the home sewer, but should only be used on very lightweight fabrics, because it tends to get very bulky. The most often used industry finish is the overedge machine finish. It is a very good substitute for the French seam. A similar finish can be achieved with a zigzag edge on a home sewing machine.

To sew seams set machine stitch for 12 to 14 stitches to the inch. Shirring or gathering requires a machine stitch of 8 to 10 stitches to the inch.

sewing plain seams

1. Plain seams are the simplest to sew. With right sides of the fabric together, match crossmarks, if any, and pin. Stitch on the seamlines. Plain seams will usually require some finish on the raw edge of the fabric, because constant wear and laundering will cause the fabric to ravel. However, plain seams that are covered, such as in a facing or inside a lining, will not require any finish.

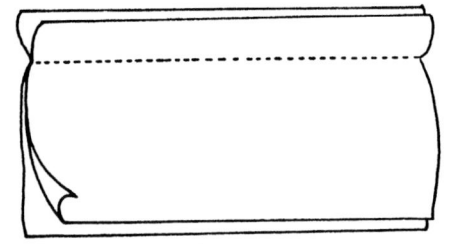

2. Loosely woven fabric can be finished with a zigzag stitch or on an overedge machine. Each side is finished separately or together depending on the weight of the fabric and the shape of the seam. For example, when joining a gathered skirt to a yoke, seams are pressed up and away from the gathers and are finished together.

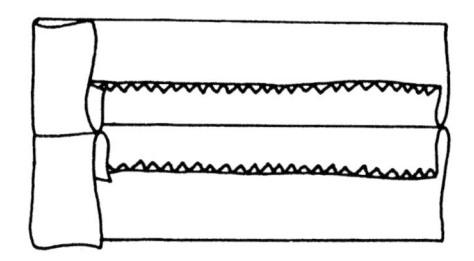

sewing french seams

French seams are best used on sheer or lightweight fabric such as organdy or voile. They completely encase the raw edges of the seam, and are good for straight or slightly curved seams.

With wrong sides of the fabric together, pin and stitch seam on right side of the fabric ¼" from edge (or one-half of finished width). Trim close to stitching. Turn and make a second seam taking up remainder of seam allowance and covering edges on other side.

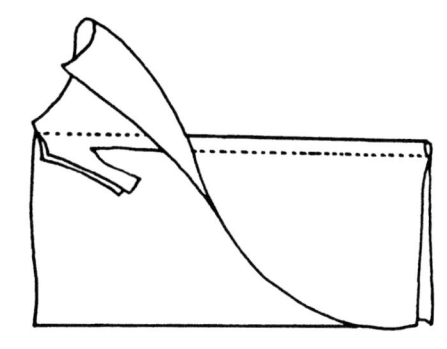

sewing flat-felled seams

Flat-felled seams can be used on light- or mediumweight fabric. They completely encase raw edges and are finished with two rows of stitching on the right side of the fabric. This seam is excellent for children's playclothes.

With wrong sides of the fabric together, stitch a plain seam. Press both seam allowances in the same direction. Trim one side of seam allowance under. Fold remaining seam allowance to ¼" over ⅛" side and topstitch close to turned edge.

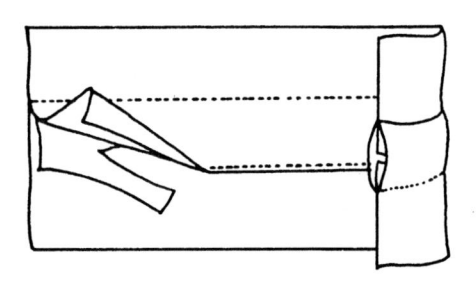

sewing intersected seams

To complete an intersected seam, stitch and finish first seam. Press open. Pin the seamed sections together matching seams. Trim first seam at corners to reduce thickness and press open.

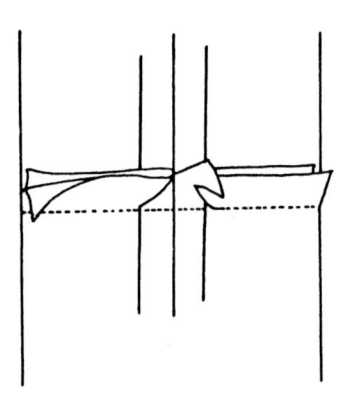

sewing facings

As discussed in the unit on PATTERNMAKING, garments will require some outside edges to be finished. Facings are one way to accomplish this finishing procedure.

sewing shaped neckline facings

1. Stitch front and back shoulder seams together. Press seam open.

2. Stitch shoulder seams of facing. Press seam open and finish outside edge with:
  A. pinked edge;
  B. zigzagged edge;
  C. or edge stitch (turn under ¼" of fabric and stitch close to edge).

3. With right sides of fabric together, pin facing to garment matching shoulder seam, center front, and center back. Stitch around neckline.

4. Trim seam allowance. Clip every ½" for round necklines; slash carefully into corners for square necklines.

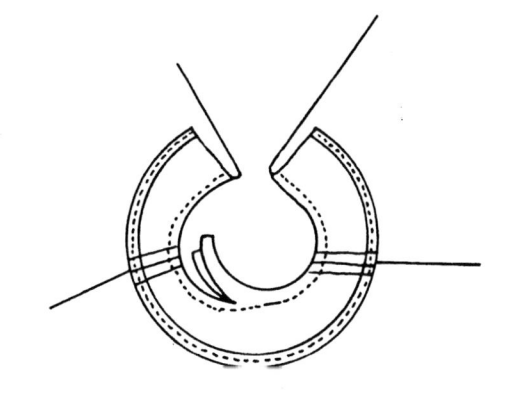

5. *BACKSTITCH* Open facing away from the main garment part. Stitch very close to the seam on the facing side of the seam, catching the seam allowances of the garment and the facing. *Backstitch* should *never* be stitched through to garment side of fabric.

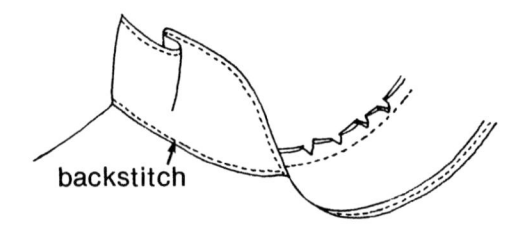

6. Tack facing to garment only at seams.

sewing back-opening facings for buttons

1. Trim facing seam allowance at center back line.

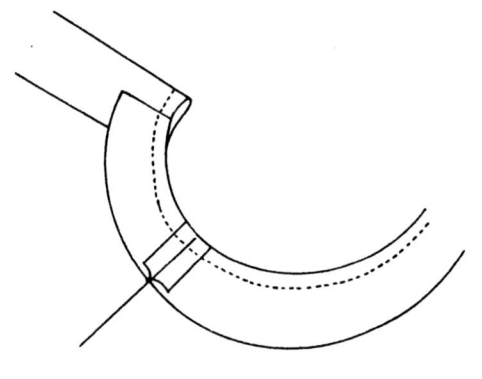

2. Fold extended facing back towards right side of fabric along extension line. Position neckline facing on top of folded facing and stitch from center back edge around neckline.

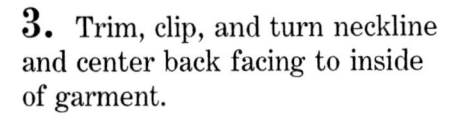

3. Trim, clip, and turn neckline and center back facing to inside of garment.

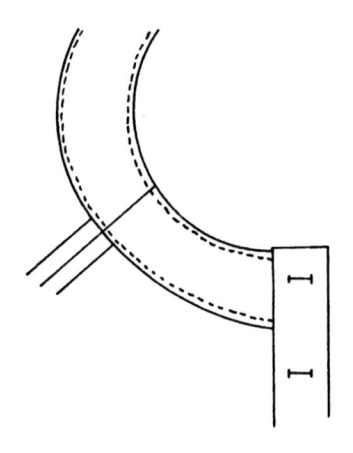

4. Follow BACKSTITCH instructions.

5. Tack facing at shoulder seams *only*.

6. See SEWING BUTTONS & BUTTONHOLES.

sewing back-opening facings for zippers

1. See SEWING SHAPED NECKLINE FACINGS, Steps 1 and 2.

2. Fold neckline facing back from center back of garment ¼″.

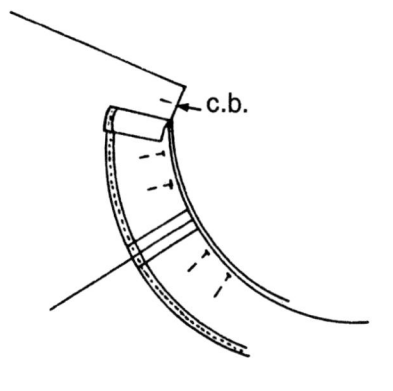

3. Fold seam allowance of garment back on center-back line over facing. Stitch neckline seam.

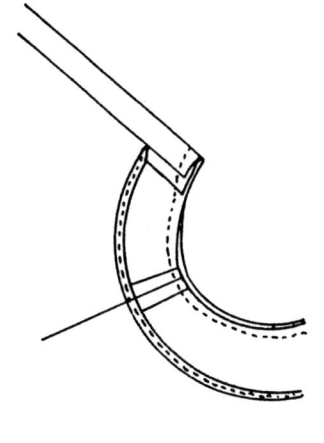

4. See SEWING BACK OPENINGS FACINGS FOR BUTTONS, Steps 3, 4, and 5.

5. See SEWING ZIPPERS.

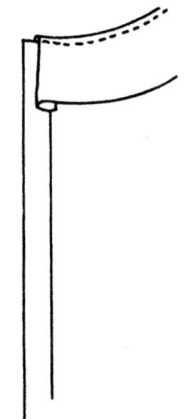

sewing armhole facings

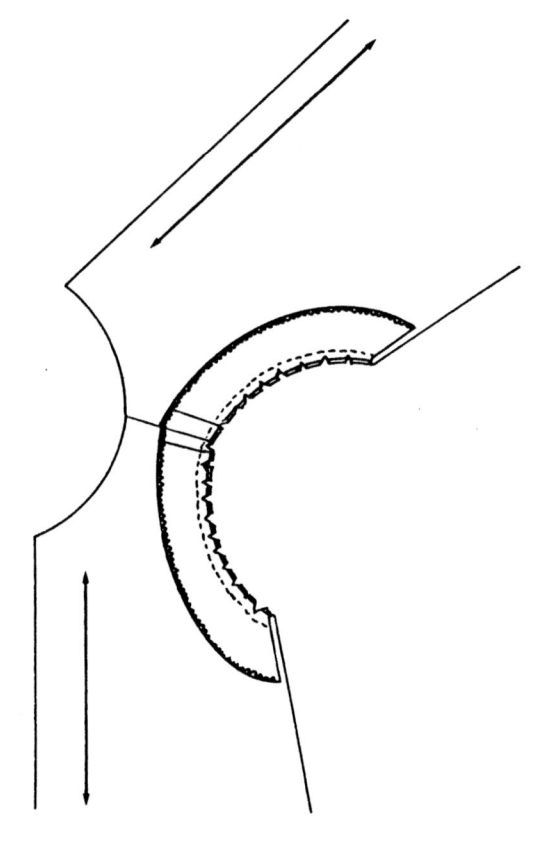

1. Stitch front and back shoulder seams of garment. Press seam open.

2. Stitch shoulder seams of facing and press seam.

3. Finish outside edge of facing as for neckline facing.

4. Keeping right sides together, match shoulder seams and armhole crossmarks.

5. Stitch, trim, and clip.

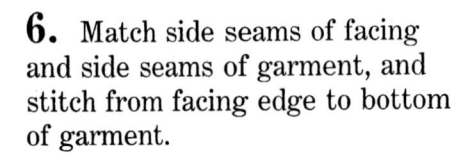

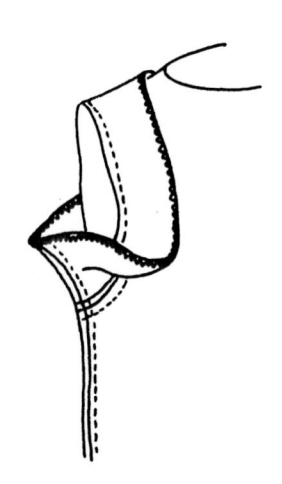

6. Match side seams of facing and side seams of garment, and stitch from facing edge to bottom of garment.

7. BACKSTITCH armhole. Tack at shoulder and side seams.

sewing one-piece neckline & armhole facings

A one-piece neckline and armhole facing is used on sleeveless garments and jumpers. When a heavyweight fabric is used, facing can be made of a lighter weight fabric.

1. See SEWING SHAPED FACINGS, Steps 1 and 2.

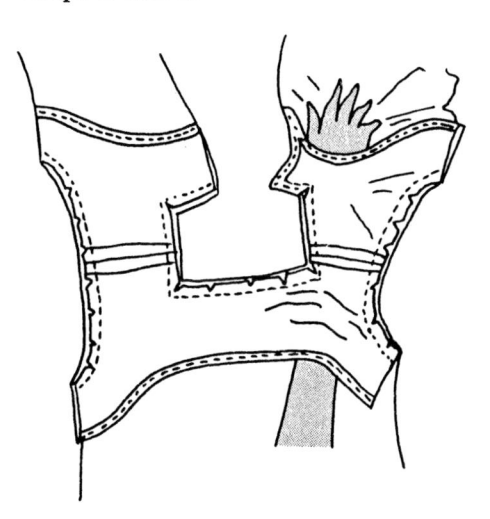

2. With right sides of fabric together, pin facing to garment matching seams and crossmarks. *Do not* stitch side seams or back seam of facing or garment. Stitch neckline and armhole seams.

3. Turn right side out by inserting hand from front between garment and facing and pulling back section through shoulder.

4. BACKSTITCH armhole and neckline facing to seam allowance whenever possible.

5. Match armhole seams. Pin and stitch from edge of facing down side seam. Press seams open. Tack facing at shoulder and side seams.

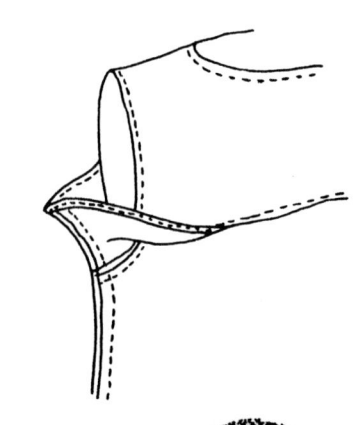

sewing facings for buttoned shoulders

A garment with buttons and buttonholes on the shoulder eliminates the need for any other closing.

1. Stitch side seams of garment and facing.

2. Pin and stitch facings to front and back. Clip curves and turn to right side.

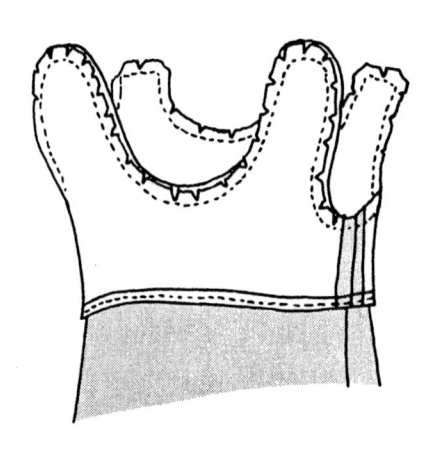

sewing collars

Collars are cut usually in two pieces: an upper- and undercollar. Some collars are cut in one piece with the collar folded in half and seamed only on the sides.

Collars on children's clothes are not always interfaced. However, collars on shirts, where a stiffer more tailored look is desired, may require interfacing. To interface a collar, cut interfacing out using collar pattern. Stitch interfacing to wrong side of undercollar on seam allowance line. Trim interfacing seam allowances very close to stitching (about $1/32$ of an inch).

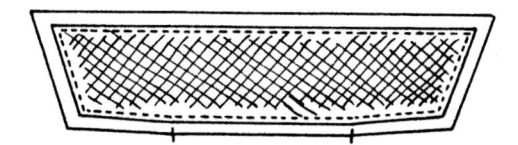

sewing peter pan collars

The Peter Pan collar can go around the neckline in one piece, if garment is open at the front. Or it can be split to accommodate a back opening.

1. Stitch under- and upper-collars together along outside edge *only*. Trim seam allowance to $1/8''$ for light- and medium-weight fabric. For heavyweight fabric, trim to $1/4''$ and clip seam allowance to facilitate turning.

2. Turn carefully (push out until seamline is on outside edge). Baste close to edge with uneven basting (small stitches on top and larger stitches on the bottom). Press.

sewing peter pan collars with trimmings

The Peter Pan collar has a sharpely curved seamline which can be difficult to sew and turn over to form a nicely rounded line. One way to overcome this problem is to insert trimming between the upper- and undercollar seams. This helps to turn the collar more neatly and to absorb any uneven stitching.

Trimmings suitable for collars include cording, rickrack, lace, eyelet, embroidered edges, and self ruffles. Flat eyelet-embroidered edges and ruffles should be shirred and pulled to desired fullness before applying to collar. This is especially important if collar has a rounded shape. Ruffles can also be cut from self or contrasting fabric (see RUFFLES). Determine whether trimming will vanish at center front (Figure 1) or meet at center front (Figure 2). If trimming will meet at center front, reduce outside edge of collar by the width of the trimming to accommodate the additional width.

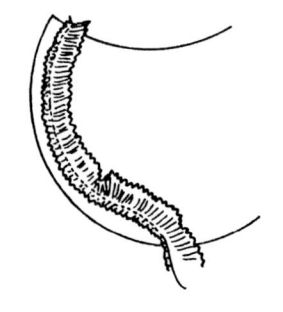

1. Pin and stitch trimming desired to right side of upper collar.

2. Place undercollar to right side of upper collar and pin. Turn collar over so you can see the first row of stitching and stitch on the same line. Trimming will be sandwiched between upper- and undercollars and will extend out when collar is turned.

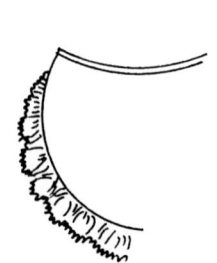

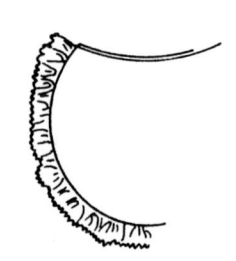

sewing peter pan collars with collar binding to garments

A collar binding is a *true bias* strip cut from the same fabric as the collar. When the fabric is too heavy, use a lighter weight fabric for the binding in a color that matches the collar fabric. See BINDINGS & PIPINGS for instructions on how to cut a true bias strip.

1. Cut strip 1 3/4" wide and long enough to go around neckline. Fold in half and press. Trim ends evenly.

2. Pin collar to neckline of garment carefully matching centers. Be sure collar *meets* exactly at center front. Stitch.

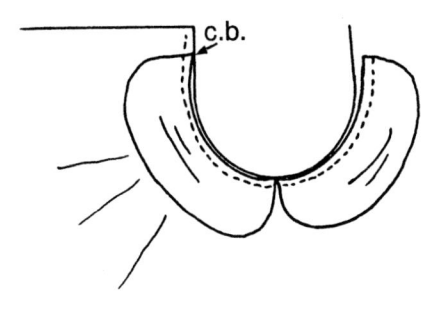

3. Turn facing or seam allowance for zipper back over collar. Pin binding slightly below collar and garment edges. Stitch.

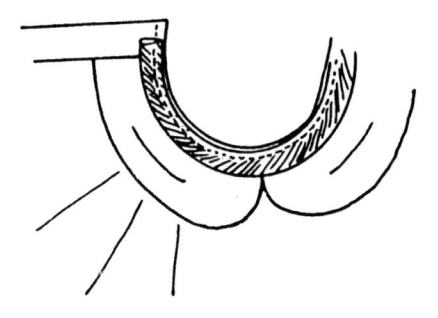

4. Trim seam allowance to ⅛" and clip carefully. For a heavy-weight fabric, layer seam allowances.

5. Hold collar out from garment with binding turned over seam allowance. Edge-stitch binding to garment. At center front stitch a tiny "V" so that stitching does not show where collars separate.

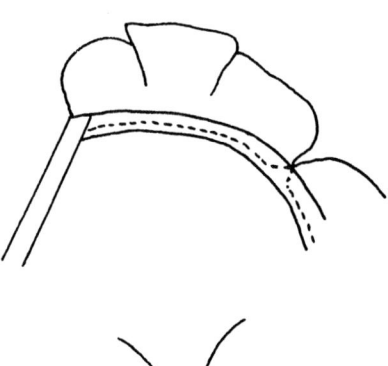

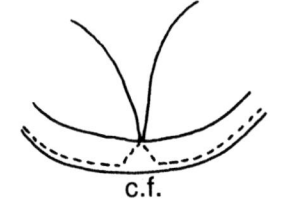

sewing mandarin or band collars

1. Prepare as for PETER PAN COLLAR WITH OR WITHOUT TRIMMING.

2. With right side of collar to wrong side of garment, fit collar to garment neckline matching crossmarks and centers. Pin and stitch. Trim seam allowance, layer if necessary.

3. Turn to right side of garment. Turn seam allowance under and baste covering first stitching line. Topstitch neatly. Pull ends of threads at center to wrong side and tie off.

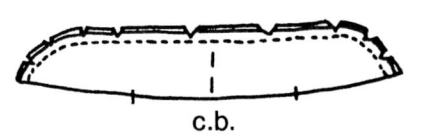

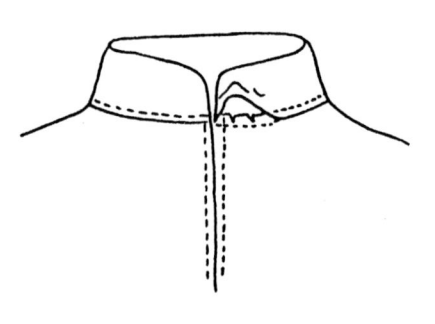

sewing convertible collars

1. Prepare as for PETER PAN COLLAR WITH OR WITHOUT TRIMMING. If this is a one-piece collar, stitch ends, trim seam allowance, clip corners, and turn.

2. Fit collar to garment neckline matching shoulder crossmarks and centers. Stitch both collar edges to garment up to shoulder seam. Clip seam allowance of collar at shoulder. Hold uppercollar away and continue stitching only undercollar to garment.

3. Turn facing back over collar on extension line and stitch up to shoulder. Trim seam allowance for front of collar only and clip (clipping corners diagonally).

4. Turn facing to wrong side. Turn seam allowance of collar under and topstitch to back of neckline. Tack facing at shoulder seams.

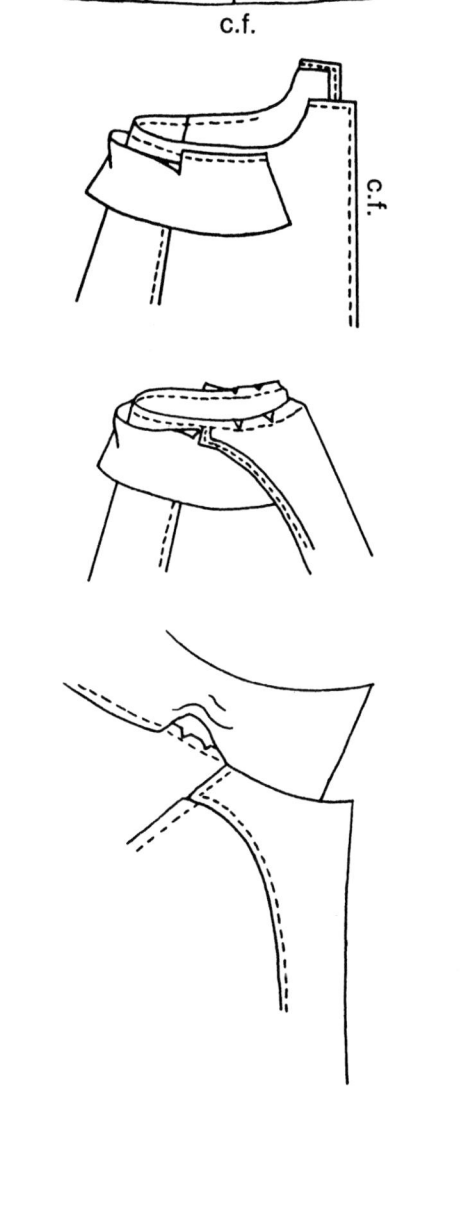

sewing two-piece shirt collars

1. Prepare convertible collar with interfacing. Topstitch collar ¼" from edges and stitch across neckline edge.

2. Interface one side of band and pin to collar matching shoulder crossmarks and centers. Pin other side of band sandwiching collar between both bands. Stitch all edges together beginning and ending ½" away from neck edge. Trim and clip seam allowance. Turn and press band away from collar.

3. Pin side of band without interfacing to neckline of shirt (right side of collar to wrong side of garment). Match shoulder crossmarks and all centers. Turn remaining band to right side of garment and seam allowance under. Pin carefully covering seam. Edge-stitch band.

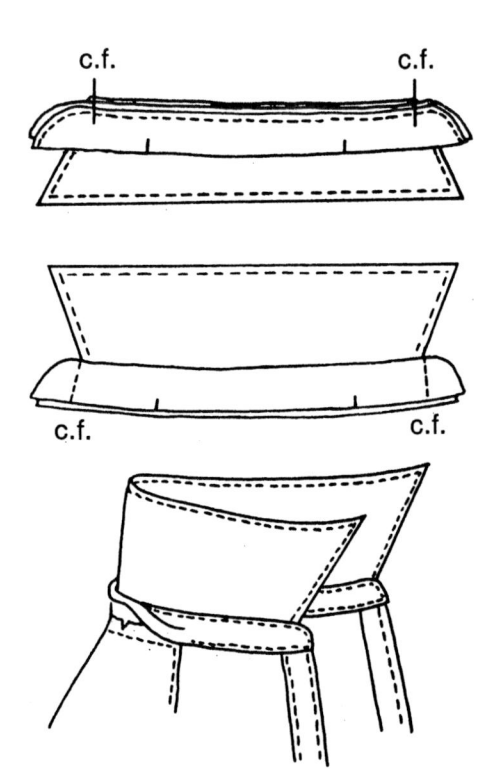

sewing sleeves

Before sewing sleeves into the garment, the bottom edges should be partially or completely finished. The type of finish to be applied will depend on the style of the sleeves. The underarm seam of the short sleeve is left open until the sleeve is sewn into the garment. The bottom third of a full-length sleeve is sewn to facilitate completing the sleeve bottom if a cuff is to be added.

sewing puffed sleeves with band cuffs

1. Set machine for shirring size stitch (8 to 10 stitches to the inch). Sew two rows of shirring on the cap and bottom edges of the sleeve. One row on the seamline, the second row ¼" away from first row in the seam allowance.

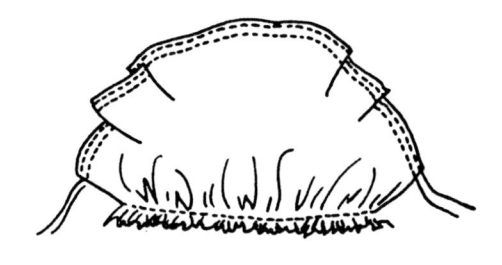

2. Determine length of band by measuring biceps of child plus ½" for ease. Pull both bottom shirring stitches to equal length of band. Distribute fullness evenly across bottom between crossmarks.

3. Stitch right side of band to wrong side of sleeve. Trim. Turn to right side, turn seam allowance under, and topstitch neatly.

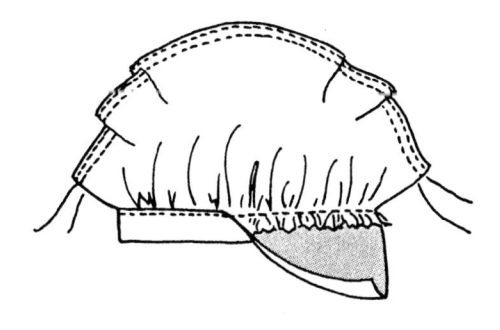

sewing sleeves with bias binding

1. Prepare bottom of sleeve as for SEWING PUFFED SLEEVES WITH BAND.

2. Cut a bias strip 1 3/4" wide and biceps measurement long. Fold and press bias strip in half. Pin bias strip to right side of shirred sleeve bottom stretching bias slightly. Use 1/4" seam allowance for binding. Adjust gathers, if necessary, and trim seam allowance to 1/8".

3. Turn binding over seam allowance to wrong side. Binding should measure 1/4" on right side. Be sure folded edge of binding extends over seamline on wrong side, stitch on right side directly on seamline. This is called *crack stitching*. See BINDINGS & PIPINGS for hand finishes.

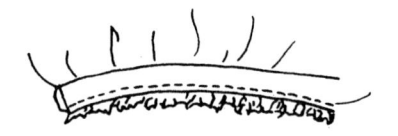

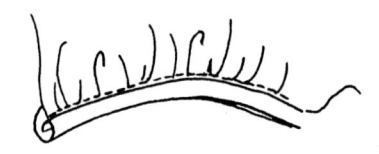

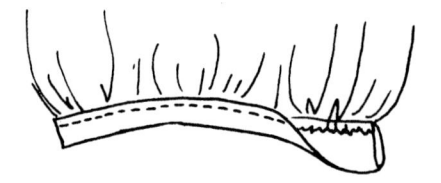

sewing sleeves with trimmings

To finish bottom edge of sleeve with trimming, such as eyelet-embroidered edge, lace, or rickrack, stitch trimming to right side of sleeve. Trim seam allowance and press trimming down. If fabric tends to ravel, zigzag seam allowance.

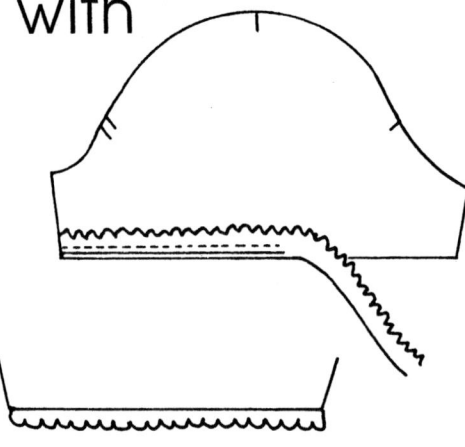

sewing sleeves with self ruffles

1. Self ruffle can be finished with trimming on bottom edge as in SEWING SLEEVES WITH TRIMMED EDGE, or with ⅛" machine-stitched hem. (Turn edge twice encasing raw edge.)

2. Cut ⅛" elastic to biceps measurement exactly, *do not* add seam allowance. Position elastic where ruffle is planned and stretch from side seam to side seam edge. Holding elastic taut from underarm seam to underarm seam, stitch elastic to sleeve in center of elastic.

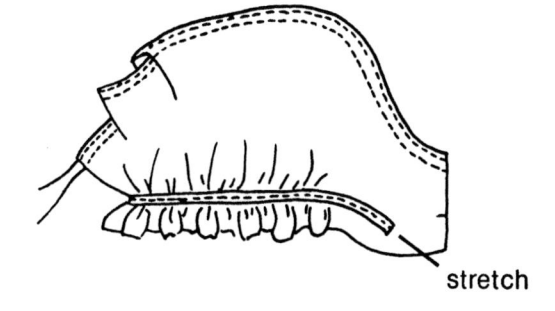

sewing sleeves with cuffs

When sleeve is finished with a cuff and an opening is needed, sew bottom half of underarm seam leaving opening for placket.

sewing faced placket openings

1. Cut a piece of self fabric 3" wide and the length of opening plus 1". Finish edges of sides and one end.

2. Position facing to garment matching center of slash and stitch marks. Starting at the bottom edge, stitch from ¼" to nothing at the top; take one stitch across, and come down on the other side. Slash.

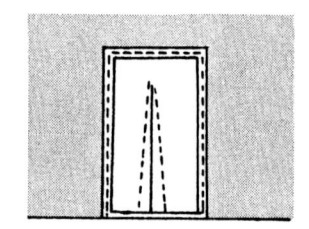

3. Turn facing to inside and press.

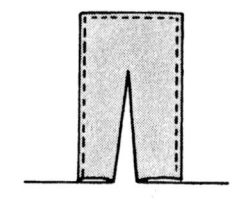

sewing continuous placket openings

1. Prepare slash by reinforcing area with machine stitch, starting from ¼" at bottom to top, take one stitch across, and down to ¼". Slash.

2. Cut a straight strip of self fabric 1½" wide and twice the length of the slash. Open edges of slash straight out and position right side of strip to wrong side of sleeve. Stitch ¼" from edge of strip in one alone along reinforced stitchline.

3. Turn strip over raw edges. Turn seam allowance under ¼" and topstitch on right side, covering first line of stitching.

4. Turn placket inside with front of placket folded back, and back of placket extended out. When cuff is closed, placket will appear as a continuation of the seam.

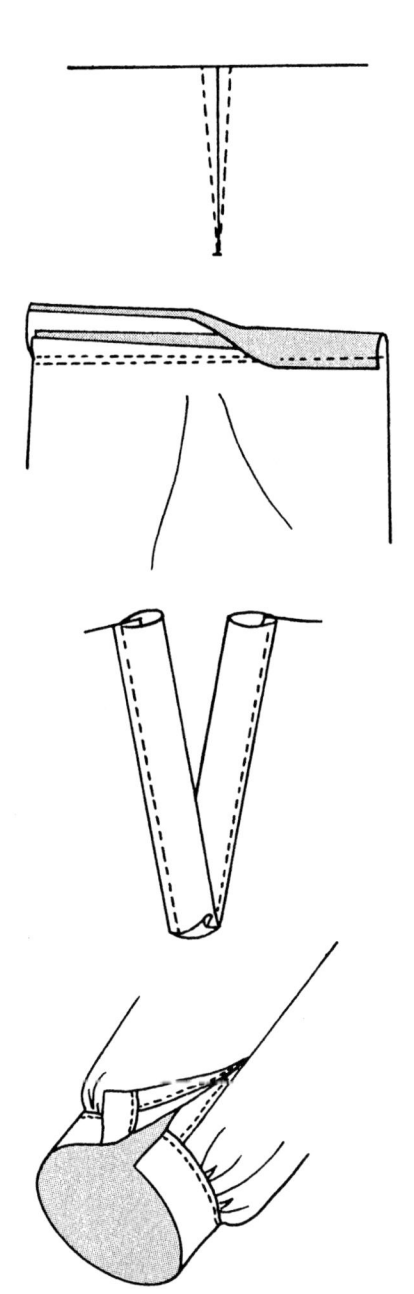

sewing false placket openings

This type of cuff can be used instead of the more complicated placket openings.

1. Cut sleeve cuff to desired width plus seam allowance. Length will equal wrist measurement plus 1½". Sew seam of cuff.

2. Sew two rows of shirring stitches around bottom edge of sleeve. Sew bottom third of underarm seam. Pull both rows of shirring stitches to fit cuff. Pin right side of cuff to wrong side of sleeve, distributing gathers evenly. Stitch.

3. Turn cuff to right side. Turn seam allowance under and edge-stitch neatly covering seamline.

4. Place buttonhole on side of cuff through all thicknesses. Sew on button. (See BUTTONS & BUTTONHOLES.)

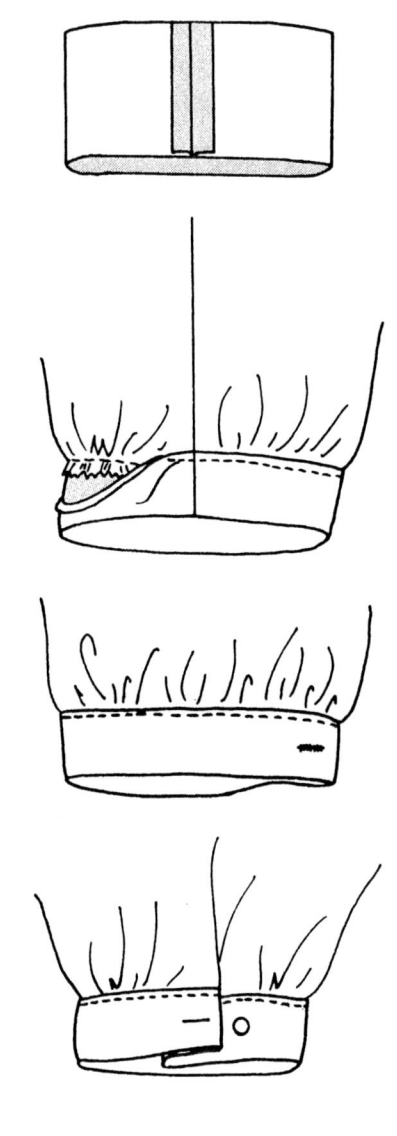

sewing sleeves with linings

Instead of facing the short-shaped sleeve, it can be made double—that is, it can be *lined*. When using a heavyweight fabric, such as velveteen or corduroy, a lighter-weight lining fabric should be used.

1. Cut four sleeves: two garment sleeves and two lining sleeves. Pin right sides of one garment and one lining sleeve together, making sure you are preparing a right and left sleeve. Stitch along bottom edge. Clip seam allowance and press open.

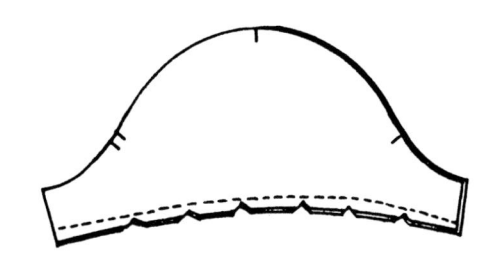

2. Fold sleeve in half, matching underarm seams. Pin sleeve and lining carefully. Stitch and press seam open.

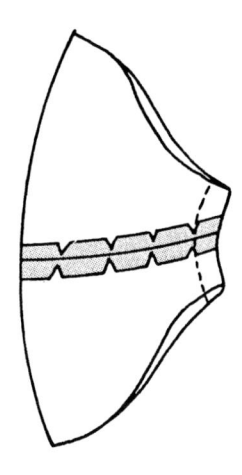

3. Turn lining to inside and baste along bottom edge, rolling lining slightly towards inside. Sew two rows of shirring stitches on cap through *both* thicknesses.

sewing sleeves into garments

The armholes on children's garment are small and to facilitate sewing, it is advised that the sleeves be sewn into the armhole on the flat. On the flat means that the side seams of the garment and the underarm seams of the sleeves are *left open*.

The bottom edges of the sleeves should be finished before the sleeves are set in.

1. Prepare bottom edges of sleeves as desired.

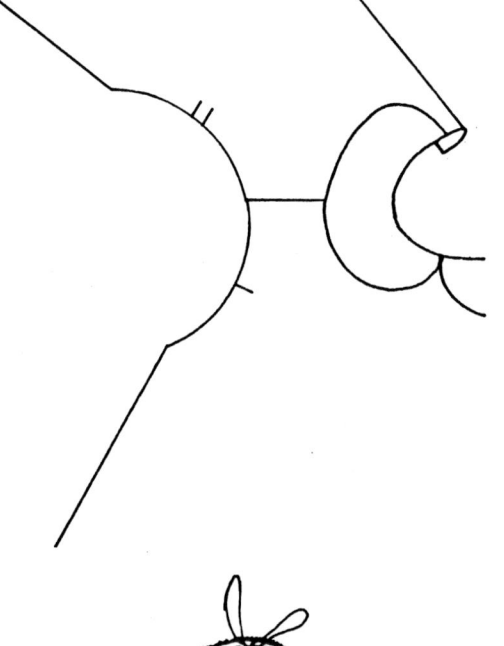

2. For a puffed sleeve, sew two rows of shirring on the cap. Pull shirring stitch at cap by inserting a pin on the bobbin side of the stitching in the center of the sleeve. Pull evenly on both rows of stitching to equal size of armhole. Distribute gathers evenly between crossmarks. *Be sure no fullness extends past the crossmarks to the underarm seam.*

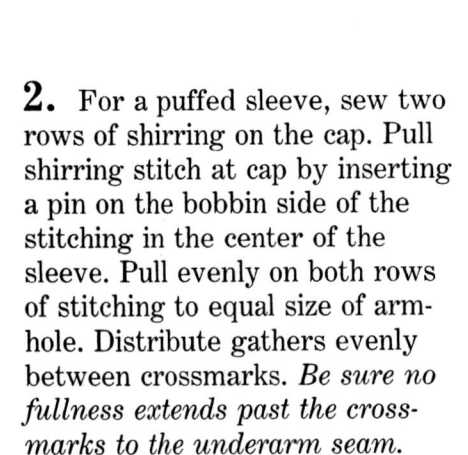

For sleeves with a flat cap, ease the fullness so that it does not lump in one spot. There should be *no* visible gathers in a flat cap, *only* ease.

3. Pin sleeve to armhole matching center of sleeve to shoulder seam and crossmarks. Stitch on sleeve side, adjusting gathers where necessary. Sew two rows of stitching; one on capline and one ¼" above the first stitchline. Trim seam allowance very close to stitching.

4. *ON LIGHT- AND MEDIUMWEIGHT FABRICS* Match armhole seam and sleeve bottom edges carefully. Stitch a small French seam from sleeve bottom to just before armhole seam. Continue seam with a plain seam down the side seam. This will provide a clean finish for the underarm area on a short sleeve.

5. *ON HEAVYWEIGHT FABRICS* Sleeve may also be finished by stitching a plain seam from sleeve bottom down side seam to hem. Trim seam allowance to ¼" from sleeve bottom to just before armhole seam and zigzag seam allowances together *in armhole area only.* Finish seamline.

6. For full-length sleeves with cuffs, follow same procedure as for pinning sleeve and stitching into armhole of garment as discussed above. Stitch a plain seam from where sleeve has been partially joined (bottom third of sleeve) down side seam to hem.

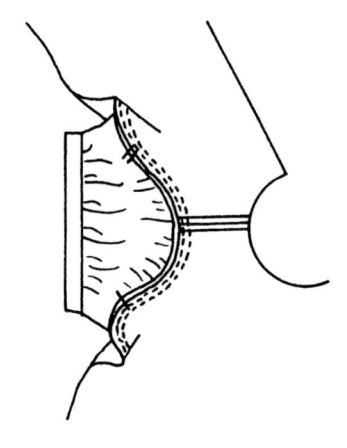

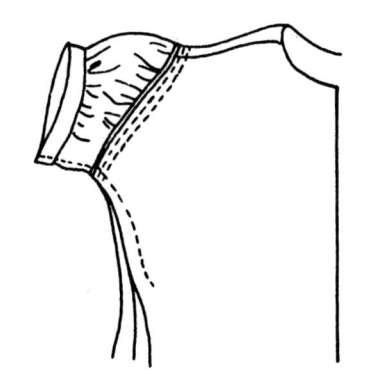

sewing yokes

Yoke designs will vary for each garment you create, and you will have to adapt different sewing methods. The yoke, which is inserted into the garment, usually is made only on the front. Regardless of the outside shape of the yoke, it will look most effective if some kind of trimming is inserted between the seams. Piping, cording, laces, etc., all help to improve the look of a garment with a yoke. This is especially true if the outside edge of the yoke is curved. Because the curved seam is difficult to sew evenly, the trimmings will tend to absorb any unevenness in the seam (see PETER PAN COLLARS WITH TRIMMING).

inserted yoke

When the yoke is separate from the skirt, the yoke will usually be planned in the front and the back. Prepare skirt section and join to yoke with rights sides of fabric together. Trimming may be inserted between the seams as for inserted yokes. Be sure you leave sufficient opening for the garment to go comfortably over the child's head (see OPENINGS & CLOSINGS).

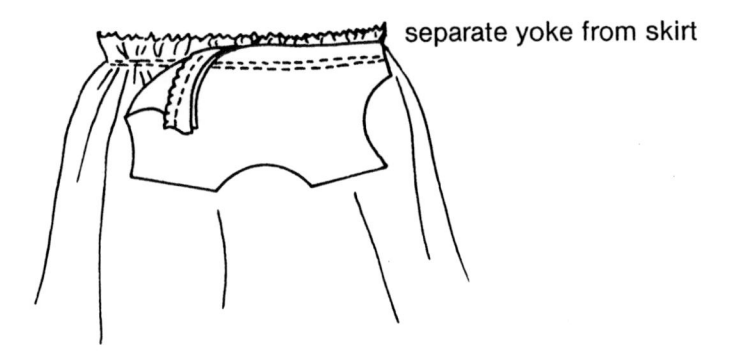

separate yoke from skirt

sewing shirts

The construction of a shirt for girls or boys is the same with this exception:

- The buttonholes are placed on the right-hand tab for girls and on the left for boys.

The shirt discussed here is made with a tab opening on the buttonhole side and a turn-back facing on the button side. Use the same pattern for both sides of the front. Plan for a one- or two-piece shirt collar (see DRAFTING COLLARS).

1. *SEWING TAB SIDE* Fold front extension twice towards wrong side of garment (fold 1″ and then again). The folded edge is now at the center front. Stitch ¼″ in from folded edge.

Turn tab out and away from garment. Topstitch on outside edge ¼″ in from fold. Raw edge will be encased and center of tab will automatically be center front of shirt.

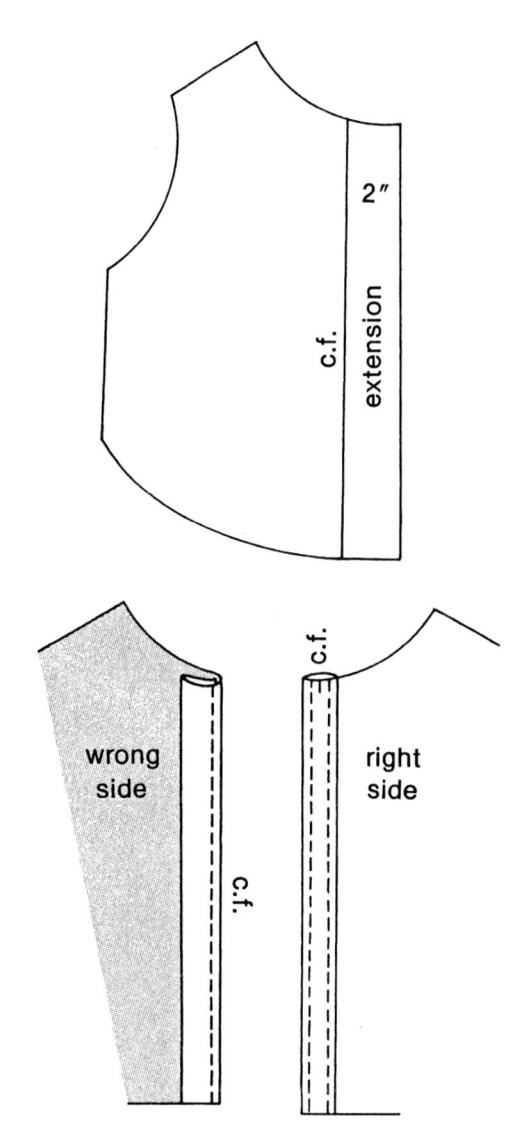

2. *SEWING FACING SIDE*
Fold edge of facing under ¼" and edge-stitch. Turn facing back to wrong side of shirt, ½" away from center front, forming a ½"-extension for buttons.

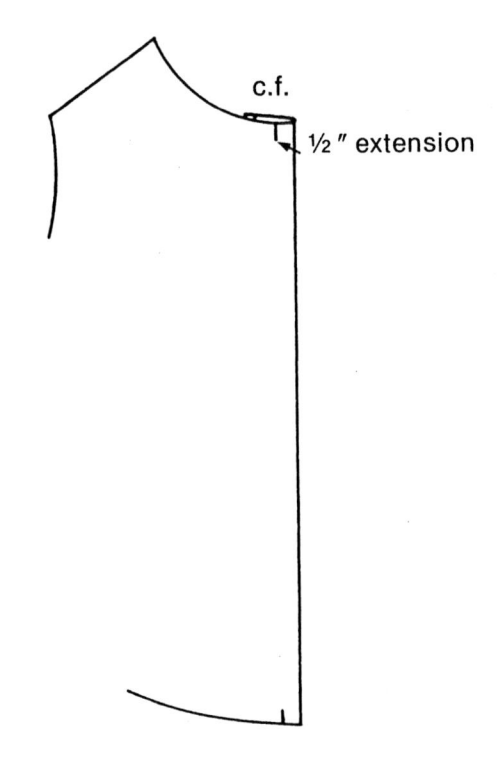

3. Finish neckline with shirt collar. Place buttonholes vertically on tab and one buttonhole horizontally on collar band.

4. To complete shirt, use a shirt sleeve. Stitch sleeves on the flat with flat-felled seams (they are neat and extra strong). Finish bottom of shirt with a machine-stitched hem. Turn ¼" twice and stitch.

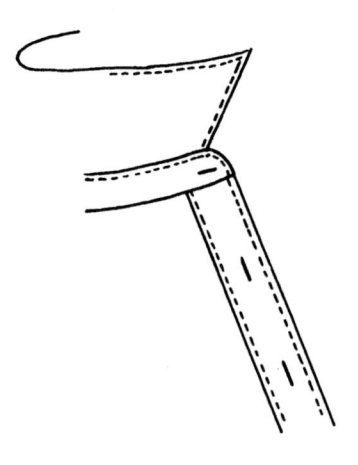

sewing skirts

1. Complete all surface decoration, such as appliqué, embroidery, or pockets before assembling skirt.

2. Skirt can be opened on the left-hand side, center front, or center back. Sew all seams leaving one seam partially open for placket or zipper. Children's skirts are often finished with a continuous placket. A 3" to 4" opening is sufficient (see SEWING SLEEVES WITH CONTINUOUS PLACKET).

3. A zipper can also be used, however, it may be difficult to find a zipper short enough and in the correct color. If you cannot find a short zipper in the correct color, use a 6" or 7" nylon skirt zipper and cut it down to 4" or 5". Measure the closed zipper from the top of the metal slide to desired length. Stitch back and forth across the zipper teeth by hand several times, forming a strong stop for the metal slide. Cut off excess length. Sew into skirt (see SEWING ZIPPERS).

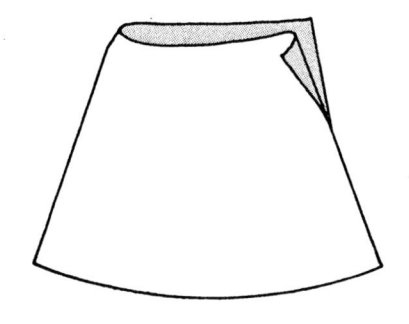

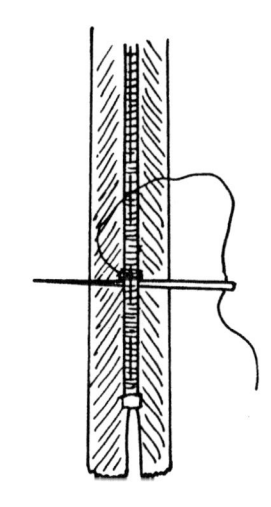

When sewing a wraparound skirt, a good way to finish it is to line it. Cut an identical skirt in lining fabric. Sew seams of outside fabric and lining. Place both pieces together, face to face. Stitch all around skirts, leaving a small opening along the hem edge for turning skirt to right side. Turn and topstitch. Place buttonholes where needed.

sewing pants

There are two methods that you can use to sew pants. Method I involves sewing the crotch seam of front and back pants, and then sewing the side seams, leaving the inseam for last. Method II involves the preparation of each pants leg separately. The crotch seam is then stitched *last*, as one long seam from front and back. Both methods can be used on either knit or woven fabrics. The second method is particularly well suited to knitted fabrics.

sewing boxer pants with elastic waistline using method I

Boxer pants are a very popular style for children, and can be made in all lengths for both girls and boys.

1. Stitch center front and center back seams using a flat-felled or inside seam. If you use an inside seam, stitch seams twice and zigzag or overedge raw edges together.

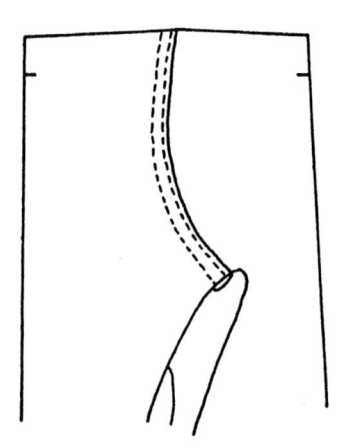

2. Stitch side seam and inseam, using the same seams as for center front and center back. When stitching inseam, match centers carefully.

3. See SEWING CASINGS FOR ELASTIC to finish casing for elastic waistline.

4. Hem pants legs to desired length.

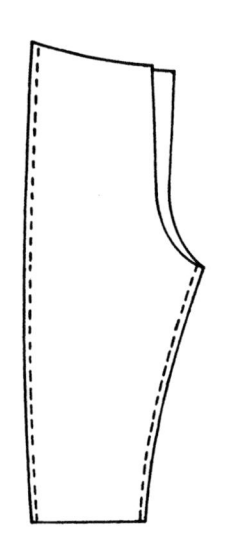

sewing boxer pants with elastic waistline using method II

1. Stitch side seam of pants, starting at the bottom of the pants leg and ending at the waistline. Repeat for other pants leg.

2. Stitch the inseam from bottom of the pants leg to crotch.

3. With right sides together, place one pants leg inside the other. Stitch crotch seam from center back waist to center front waist in one long seam.

4. See SEWING CASINGS FOR ELASTIC.

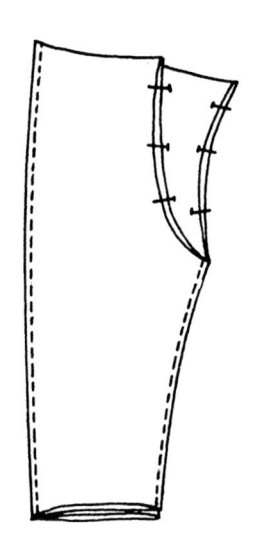

sewing pants with fly-front openings

1. Complete sewing zipper with fly-front opening (see SEWING ZIPPERS).

2. Stitch approximately 1½" of crotch seam under zipper.

3. To complete project see SEWING BOXER PANTS WITH ELASTIC WAISTLINE USING METHOD II.

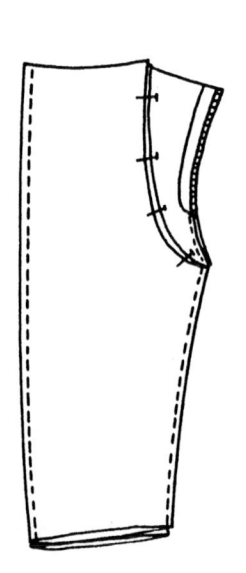

sewing pants with one-piece fly-front zipper closing

1. Finish outside edge of fly-front extension with zigzag stitch.

2. Place zipper face down on left-hand side of pants front. Edge of zipper teeth should be approximately ¼" from center front crossmark. Stitch in center of zipper tape.

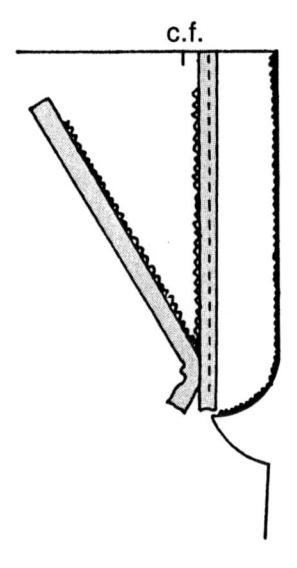

3. Turn zipper so that face side is up and stitch another row on right-hand side close to folded edge. This will encase and reinforce the zipper. A tiny pleat will form at the end of the zipper.

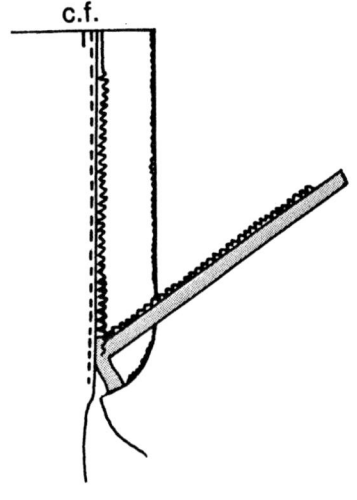

4. Position right-hand front of pants over left with right sides together. Pin zipper in place, matching center front crossmarks and crotch seam. Stitch zipper to right side of extension on zipper side. Stitch crotch seam.

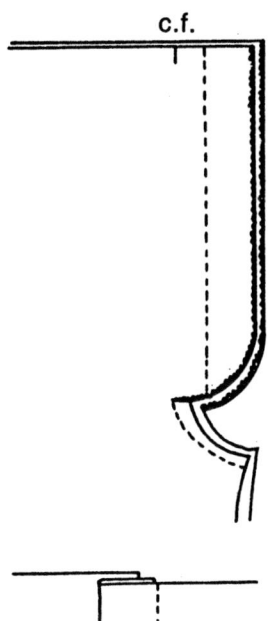

5. Turn pants to right side. Close zipper; crease right side of pants on center front from waistline to crotch seam. Stitch about 1¼″ from center front, forming a curve into the crotch and tack. Be careful to turn left-hand side extension back when topstitching so as not to catch it in final stitch.

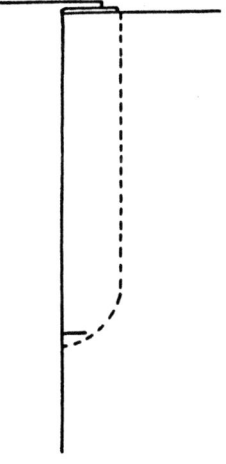

sewing pants with trouser pockets

1. Sew pocket facing to pocket edge with right sides together. Trim and slash seam allowance. Turn facing to wrong side. Topstitch ¼" from edge.

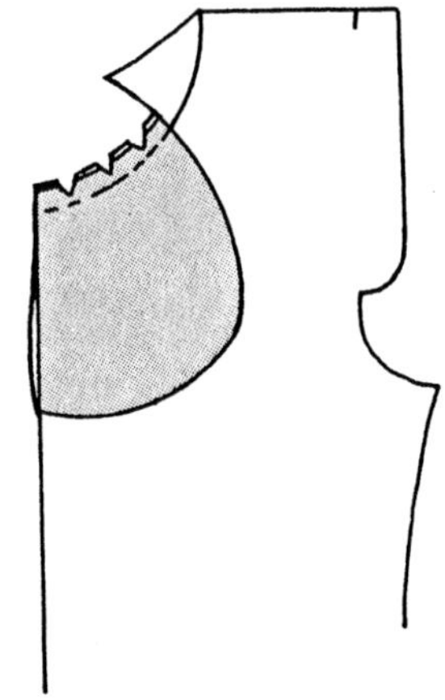

2. Position pants on smaller hip pocket section, matching waist and side seam crossmarks. Pin and stitch pocket sections together. Two rows of stitching and a zigzag-stitch for outside edge are recommended. Pin and stitch all three sections together at waistline and side seam.

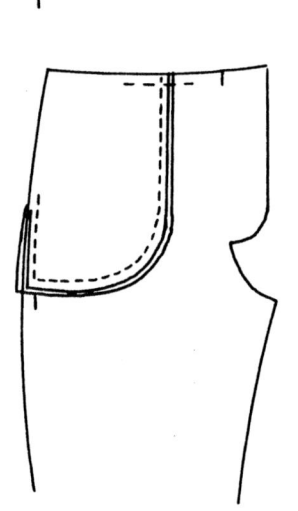

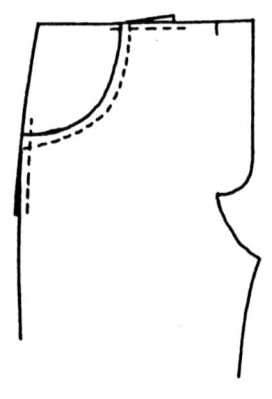

sewing pants with front waistband & elastic back

1. Prepare pants by sewing center seams, fly-front, pockets, etc.

2. Fold waistbands with right sides together. Stitch ends in desired shape. Trim and turn.

3. Sew waistband to wrong side of front. Finish on right side with topstitching.

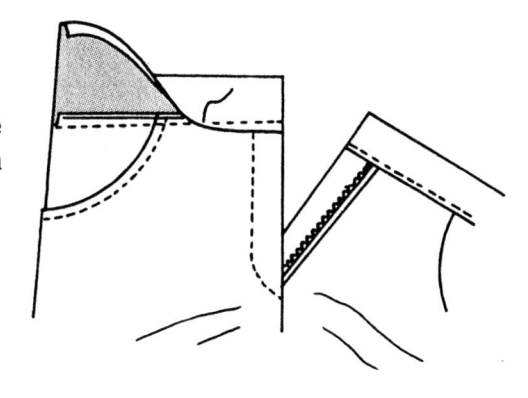

4. To finish edge of back casing, turn under ¼" and stitch. Place right sides of pants together, matching side seams. Front waistband should align with foldline of casing.

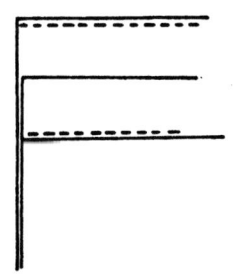

5. Turn casing down *over* waistband. Place elastic in center of casing and stitch side seam, catching waistband, casing, and elastic. Backstitch once or twice to secure, and continue stitching down side seam to pants hem. Repeat for other side seam.

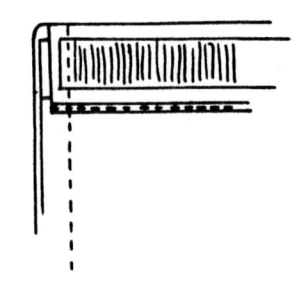

6. Turn and stitch casing to back of pants. Elastic will be encased and clean-finished.

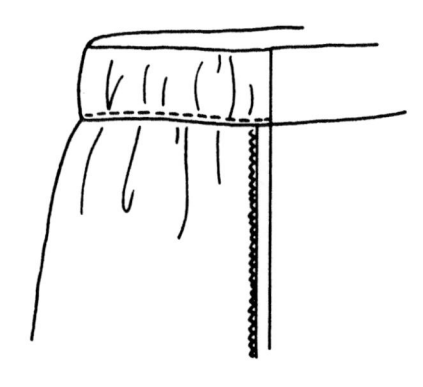

sewing waistbands

The preparation and sewing of waistbands is the same for both *skirts* and *pants*. You can adapt the following method as needed. This method will also work for preparing bands for the hems of knee pants or ankle pants, where pants legs are gathered into bands.

1. For thin fabrics, interface one-half of band. Cut interfacing ½" wider than half of the band and machine-stitch close to edges.

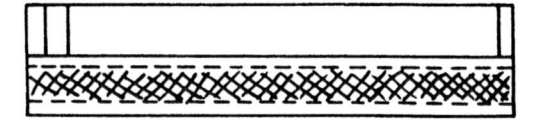

2. Fold waistband with right sides together. Stitch ends at seam allowance lines. One end will extend for closing.

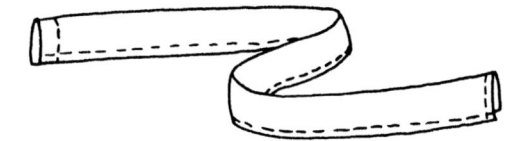

3. Sew right side of waistband to wrong side of skirt (pants), matching centers and side seams. Turn to right side. Fold seam allowance of band under and topstitch close to the folded edge. Finish with button and buttonhole or hook and eye.

sewing casings for elastic

The method of sewing a casing for elastic can be used on both skirts and pants. An elastic casing can *also* be used at the bottom of a shirt or blouse to create a blouson effect.

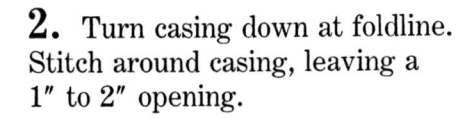

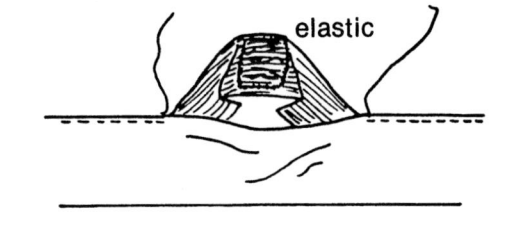

1. Turn raw edge of casing under at waistline ¼".

2. Turn casing down at foldline. Stitch around casing, leaving a 1" to 2" opening.

3. Cut elastic ½" longer than body measurement. Pull one end of elastic through casing with a safety pin. Be careful not to let elastic twist inside casing. Lap ends of elastic ½" and tack securely. Stitch casing opening.

sewing hems

A hem is a necessary finish at the bottom of all garments. The following discusses both hand- and machine-finished hems. Many times hems on children's wear are machine-stitched, especially playclothes.

1. To finish a *straight hem* as on a gathered skirt, measure up amount of hem evenly. Pin and turn up hem, matching centers and side seams. Turn under ¼" at raw edge and edge-stitch. Finish with hemming stitch. Place stitches approximately ½" to ¾" apart, picking up only one thread on garment and a little more on hem. Stitches should not be visible on face of garment. Press.

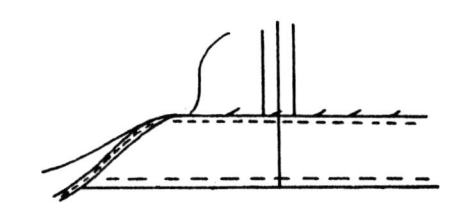

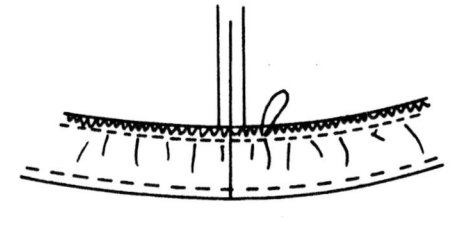

2. To finish a hem on a *bias* skirt, measure up amount of hem evenly. Pin and turn up hem evenly, matching centers and side seams. Zigzag or overedge the raw edge. Machine-stitch a shirring stitch ¼" from finished edge. Pull shirring stitch *slightly*, evenly distributing fullness across hem. *Do not* let fullness bunch in one place. Be careful not to pull hem smaller than body of garment. Finish with a hemming stitch as in Step 1.

3. *MACHINE-STITCHED HEM* Width of hem may vary from ¼" to ½" finished. Plan for finished width plus ¼" for turn-under. Turn under all around and stitch. A second stitch can be added at hem edge for double-needle effect.

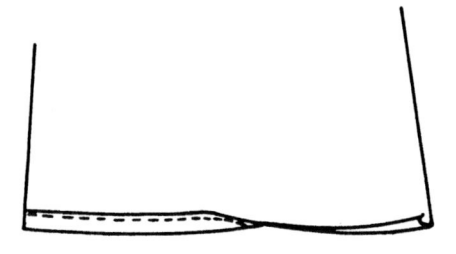

sewing buttons & buttonholes

The use of buttons and buttonholes is one of the best ways to close children's garments. Buttonholes should be machine-made, as they tend to be the strongest. It is important to know the size of the button *before* planning buttonholes. Most children's garments use a ⁵⁄₈" button, or smaller.

Plan horizontal buttonholes from the center line into the garment, and vertical buttonholes directly on the center line. To determine placement of button, overlap centers and pin through the center of one buttonhole. Sew buttons directly on center line.

There are two types of buttons:

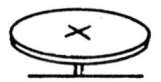

1. sew-through button (with two or four holes);
2. shank button.

Sew buttons with double thread for extra hold. For sew-through buttons, leave a little space between button and garment to allow for a stem, and for button to slide easily through buttonhole. For a shank button, sew button on with overcast stitch.

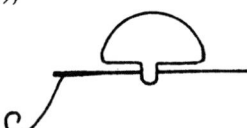

sewing snaps

Another good closing for children's garments is *dot snaps*. They hold well and are particularly well-suited to playclothes. Regular snaps will not substitute for buttons and buttonholes or dot snaps. They tend to open up and are not recommended.

sewing zippers

Select a zipper in the correct length, color, and weight for the fabric of the garment.

Prepare garment by stitching seam, leaving seam open the correct amount for zipper. Tack seam. Opening in garment should measure the length of the zipper from top stop to bottom stop.

When preparing a neckline opening, add 3/8" to zipper length for hook and eye at neckline. Also, attach facings before inserting zipper (see FACINGS). For a skirt or pants opening, plan zipper to start ½" down from raw edge so that when waistband is applied there will be no space between band and zipper.

sewing slot for centered zipper

Zipper is centered at seamline and stitched evenly on either side of opening.

1. Baste opening. Position closed zipper face down, over seamline on wrong side of garment. Baste zipper to garment.

2. Stitch on right side of garment zipper tape. Starting from top stitch down to just below metal stop. Stitch across and up the other side. Remove basting and press lightly.

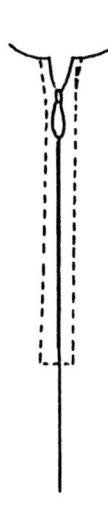

sewing seams for lapped zipper

Zipper is hidden under a lapped seam and only one row of stitching is visible.

1. Prepare garment as for centered zipper, but *do not* baste opening. Zipper will always lap from front to back on left-hand side of openings in skirts and pants. For back openings, the lap-over is on the right-hand side.

2. On underlap side of opening, fold seam allowance back 3/8" and baste.

3. With closed zipper face up, position folded edge of fabric close to zipper teeth and baste. Stitch (moving slide up and down, as necessary, to facilitate stitching). Continue stitching down to bottom of zipper tape in seam allowance.

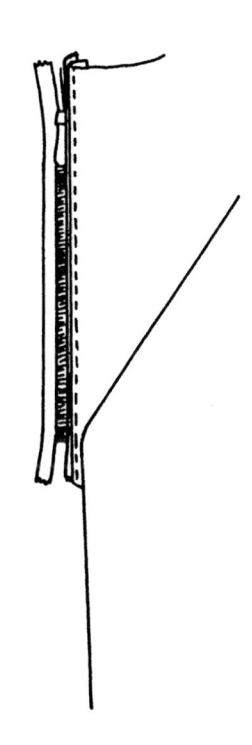

4. Fold other side of opening back ½" and align over underlap. Folded edge will automatically cover first row of stitching by ⅛". Baste and stitch (moving slide up and down, as necessary, to facilitate stitching).

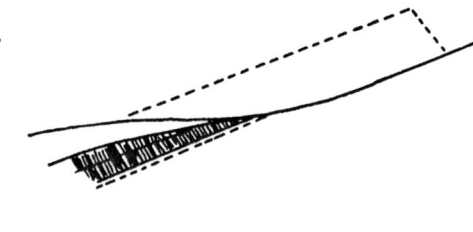

5. Finish by stitching across bottom of zipper under metal stop. *Do not tack seam.* Pull top thread to back and tie in a *tailor's knot.* To form a tailor's knot, hold two threads together and form a loop. Pull both threads through the loop and form a knot close to the base at stitching line. Inserting a pin in loop helps to pull the knot close to the stitching. Clip off threads.

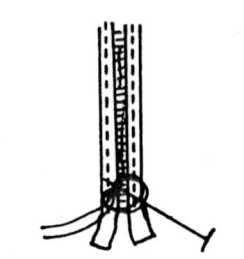

inserting zipper into slashed opening on woven fabrics

1. If there is no center back or center front seam and an opening is needed, a slashed opening is used. Measure length of slash as for zipper opening.

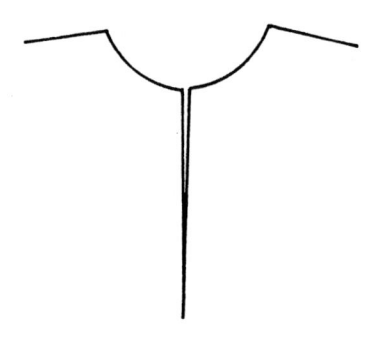

2. Reinforce slash. Stitch ⅛" from outside edge around slash, forming square corners at end of slash. Slash diagonally into corners. Turn under seam allowance.

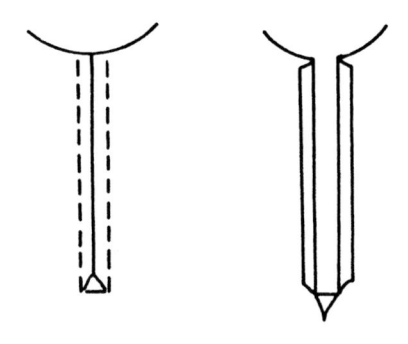

3. If fabric is very loosely woven, end of slash may need additional reinforcement. Cut a small square of fabric. With right sides together position fabric over end of slash and stitch. Slash diagonally into corners and turn.

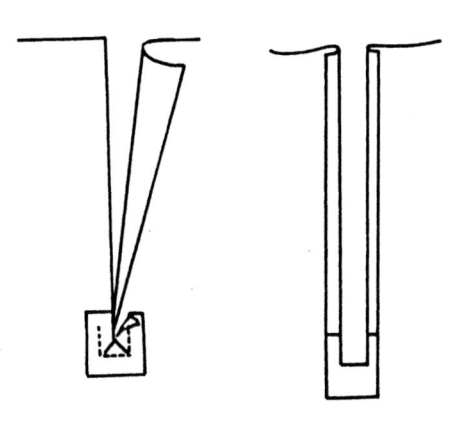

4. Prepare slash with either method and turn seam allowance under, so that opening is the width of the zipper teeth. Center zipper with teeth exposed. Baste and stitch.

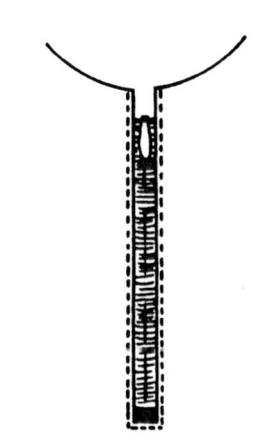

inserting zipper into slashed opening on knit fabrics

1. Position right side of zipper to right side of fabric ¼″ below slash opening. Zipper is facing away from slash. Stitch width of zipper to secure.

2. Flip zipper up to correct position. Fold one side of slash over zipper with right sides together and stitch as close as possible to zipper teeth. Repeat on the other side. Pull threads to wrong side and use tailor's knot to secure bottom. Turn to right side and press lightly.

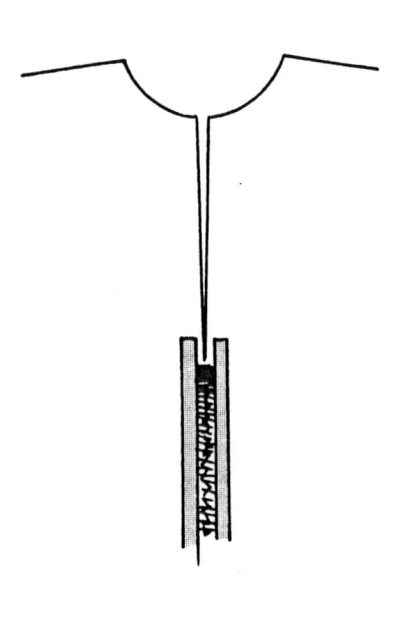

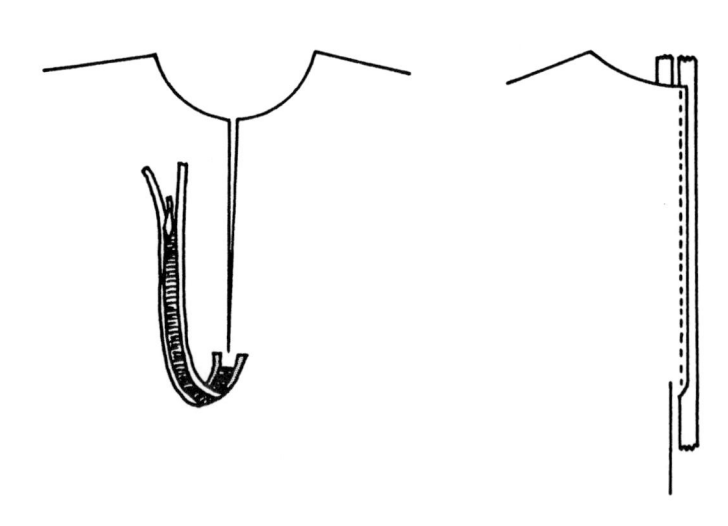

UNIT FIVE
ADDITIONS & TRIMMINGS

Lace, eyelet-embroidered edges, bindings, pipings, ruffles, appliqués, surface embroidery, etc., are all basic trimmings used in children's wear design. Not only do they make interesting variations on garments, but they are a wonderful ways to express your creativity.

Original appliqués, for example, can be planned from children's drawings or simply by combining shapes. Young children's coloring books are good sources of basic shapes which adapt well to appliqué as well as to embroidery.

Other types of trimmings include pockets, flaps and tabs, bows, and topstitching.

ruffles

Ruffles can be planned as part of an original garment or added to the bottom of an outgrown skirt or sleeve for extra length. Since ruffles are purely decorative they should be as pretty as possible. Therefore, ruffles should be cut on the lengthwise grain or the true bias. Ruffles cut on the cross grain are not attractive. Ruffles are always gathered (see GATHERS for determining amount of fullness needed). Set machine for 8 to 10 stitches to the inch. Stitch two rows of shirring stitches ¼" apart at shirring line. A shirring foot attachment is especially useful for this purpose.

ruffles on an inside seam

1. Cut ruffles to desired length and width. Some ruffles will require seaming to achieve the proper length. Finish one side of ruffle with a turned hem (edge turned twice) or use hemming attachment for ⅛" hem. A trimming edge can also be used for a finish (see SEWING SLEEVES WITH TRIMMINGS).

2. Pin and baste ruffle to garment section, adjusting gathers where necessary. Stitch ruffle to garment section on ruffle side. If fabric ravels easily, finish seam with a zigzag-stitch. Turn both seam allowances away from ruffles.

ruffles with a heading

Finish *both* edges of this type of ruffle with hems or trimmings. Shirr and stitch this ruffle onto the *outside* of the garment area to be finished.

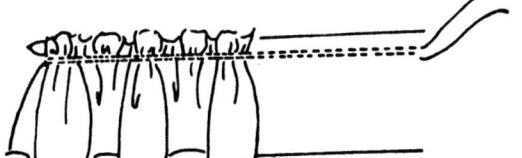

pinafore ruffles

Determine finished length of a pinafore ruffle by measuring area from front to back and adding desired amount for fullness. Shape ends (as illustrated). Finish straight edge with hem or trimmings. Gather curved side and insert into garment.

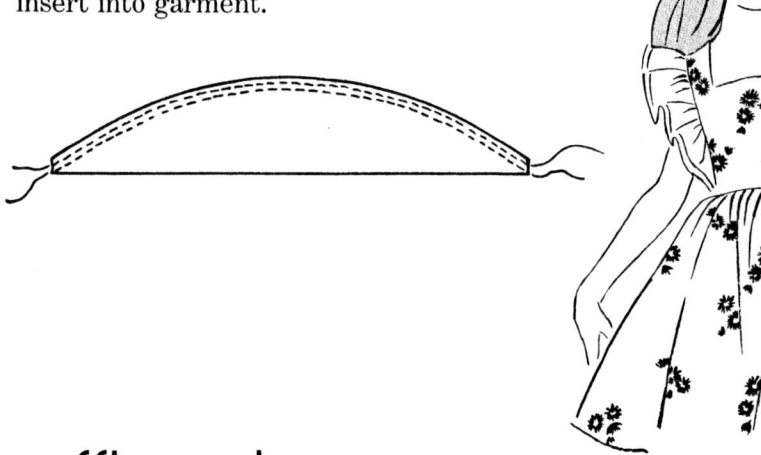

ruffles at neckline & armhole

Ruffles at the neckline and armhole are generally small—about ½" to 1" wide—and can be cut on the straight or bias. If very sheer fabric is used, ruffle can be made double eliminating the need for a finish on the outside edge. Seam allowance on necklines and armholes can be finished with a zigzag-stitch or bias binding (see SEWING COLLARS).

piping & binding

Piping and binding are strips of bias fabric used as finishes and decorations on various parts of garments such as on necklines and armholes. They can also be used to outline areas that you may wish to accentuate, such as pockets and collars. Since these finishes are cut separately and are added to the garment, they can be made in the same fabric or in contrasting fabrics and colors.

Pipings and bindings are *always* cut on the *true bias* of the fabric. They usually look best when pressed and slightly stretched before their application to the garment. French piping is a double thickness and is recommended for light- and mediumweight fabrics.

preparing bias strips

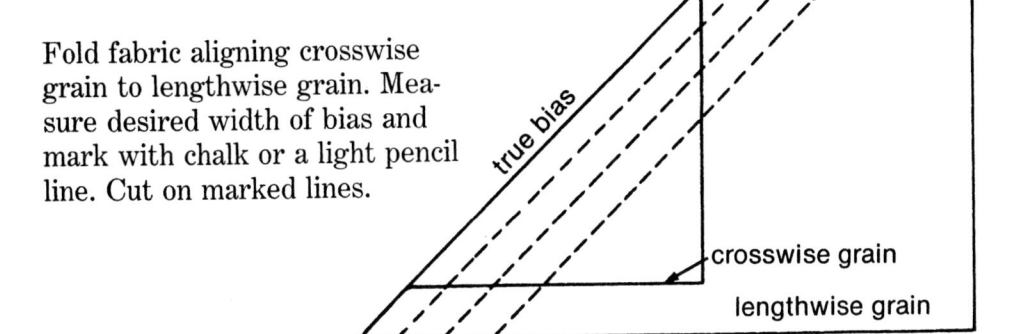

Fold fabric aligning crosswise grain to lengthwise grain. Measure desired width of bias and mark with chalk or a light pencil line. Cut on marked lines.

WIDTH OF BIAS

- For *single binding* multiply desired finished width by two and add ¼" for stretch and ½" for seam allowance. Example: ¼" binding—cut bias 1¼".

- For *French piping* multiply desired finished width by four and add ¼" for stretch and ½" for seam allowance. Example: ¼" piping—cut bias 1¾".

LENGTH OF BIAS

- Measure length of area to be bound and allow 1" to 2" more for finishing ends where necessary.

joining bias strips

With right sides together, match the two diagonal ends and stitch, taking up ¼" seam allowance. Press seam open and trim corners.

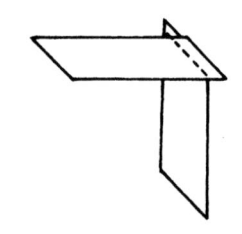

single binding

1. Prepare bias strips. Fold in half and press. Turn ¼" seam allowance towards center on right side of fabric.

2. Open binding, and with right sides together stitch to garment. Turn binding over seam allowance to wrong side and hem to garment, just barely covering stitching line.

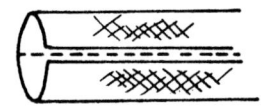

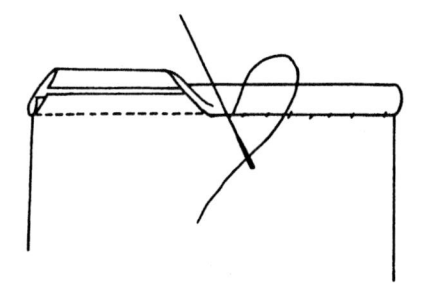

french piping

1. Prepare bias strips. Fold in half and press. Stitch to garment with right sides together.

2. Turn to wrong side and hem as for binding.

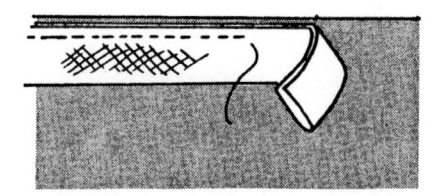

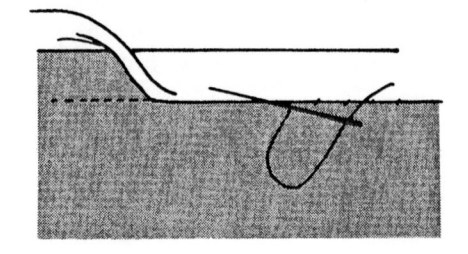

finishing binding & piping

Both bindings and pipings can be finished by machine and are *always* machine-finished on commercially made garments.

1. Follow instructions for either binding or piping to hemming step.

2. Turn folded edge to wrong side, being careful that folded edge extends slightly past stitching line. Use a *crack-stitch* on right side exactly on the seamline. When matching thread is used and stitching is done carefully, stitch will disappear into seam and be almost invisible.

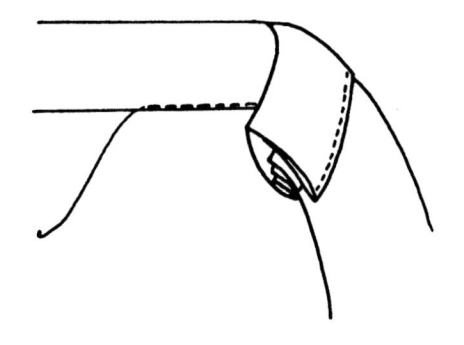

cording

Cording is used in a seam for accent or on a collar or yoke as a finish. Use very narrow cord—1/16" to 1/8"—is best on children's clothing. Cut bias strip about 1" and encase cording in bias strip by sewing very close to cord with a zipper foot. To stitch cording to garments, see SEWING COLLARS.

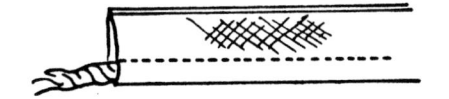

string or spaghetti ties

String ties can be used as straps, bows, and trimmings. When made very narrow, they also serve for button loops.

Cut bias strip to length and four times the finished width desired. Fold in half and stitch in center of strip on wrong side of fabric. Leave ends open for turning. A loop turner is available in some notions departments and simplifies turning. However, if a loop turner is not available, attach a needle with double thread to one end of strip and slip into opening with eye of needle going in first. Pull to turn.

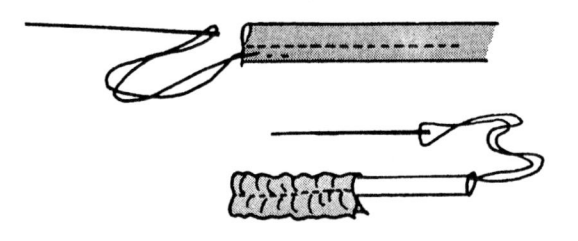

appliqué & embroidery

Appliqué and embroidery can enhance a garment just as frosting enhances a cake. However, unlike a cake these trimmings should be planned and completed before sewing the garment together. Whether you are planning machine or hand appliqué or embroidery, an advantage to completing the unassembled section is that in case of a mishap the one section can be recut without having to redo the entire garment. It is also much easier to embroider or appliqué a small section rather than a finished garment.

Appliqués are pieces of fabric, which are cut in shapes and sewn into the garment. The secret of a successful appliqué, as well as successful embroidery, on children's clothing is to keep the design simple. Geometric shapes, animals, fruits, and flowers make excellent motifs for designs.

Color and fabric are very important, also, so plan carefully. Use only washable materials for appliqués. Firmly woven fabrics are easiest to work with, but should be of a similar weight to the garment fabric.

machine-made appliqué

Cut out desired shape with ¼" seam allowance all around. Pin to garment and machine-stitch on seamline. Trim seam allowance very close to stitching. Zigzag-stitch around outside edge with matching or contrasting thread.

If fabric to be appliquéd is very thin, double it or back it with a firmer fabric. Press-on fabric can be used and eliminates the need for the first stitching process in applying an appliqué. Press on and zigzag edges as above.

handmade appliqué

Follow method as for machine-made appliqués, but use a *blanket stitch* around edges instead of a zigzag-stitch.

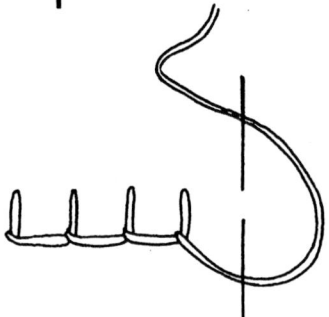

belts & sashes

When planning the length of a belt or sash, be sure to consider what type of closing will be used. For example, a bow will require more fabric than a knot or a buckle. A belt which is to go around the body will have to be longer than one that is to be inserted into the sides seams of a garment. Tie a tapemeasure around the child's waistline to determine a belt measurement.

sashes

Sashes are belts made of single pieces of fabric and finished on all edges with a very narrow hem—⅛" to ¼". A narrow hem attachment for your sewing machine is excellent for this design feature.

1. Stitch one long side of the sash with the narrow hem attachment, or turn the edge under twice and stitch.

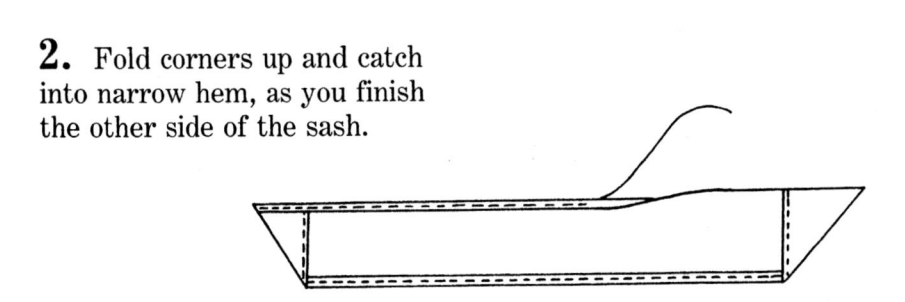

2. Fold corners up and catch into narrow hem, as you finish the other side of the sash.

Sashes attached to side seams of a garment are made the same as full-length sashes, but in two pieces. Finish each sash section separately, and gather at one end. Stitch each section into the respective side seam *before* stitching side seam of garment.

belts

A belt can be made by folding the fabric in half and stitching around, leaving an opening in the center of approximately 2" for turning. This type of belt usually finishes at approximately 1" to 1½" wide.

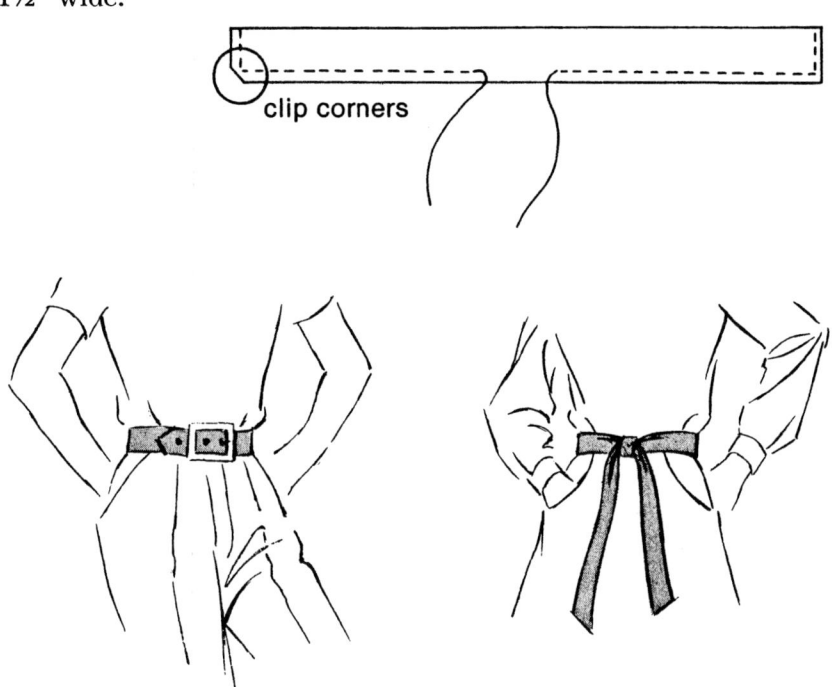

clip corners

ADDITIONS & TRIMMINGS/BELTS & SASHES

pockets

Pockets stitched on top of a garment are called *patch pockets*. They are simple to make and kids love them. Always determine size and placement of pocket on garment by having child try on garment. Proportion and placement can make or break your garment. These illustrations show the three classic pocket shapes, and how you can vary the design with topstitching or appliqués and embroidery.

Pockets can also be made into cute and interesting shapes. As discussed previously, coloring books will usually have easy shapes, which adapt well to pockets.

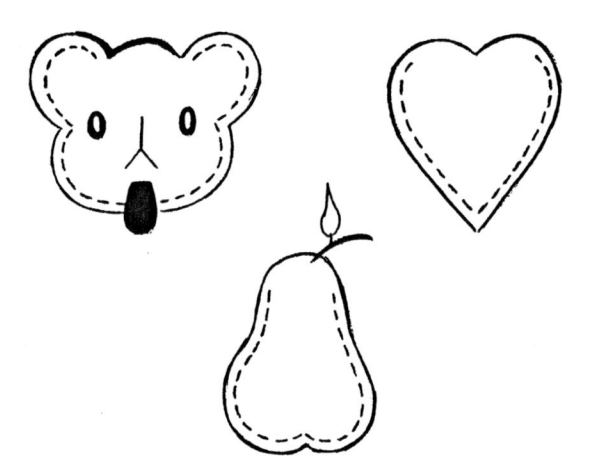

For pockets with a straight-top edge, plan a fold-back facing of approximately 1".

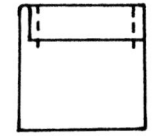

If fabric is very thin or if pocket is an unusual shape, make pocket double by stitching two identical pieces together leaving a small opening at the bottom for turning. The pocket can then be topstitched to the garment as for single pocket.

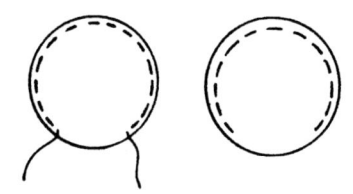

When fabric is heavyweight, use a thin fabric for lining or make a facing for open edge only. Turn under all other edges ½" and topstitch to garment. Seam allowances of pockets should be basted before stitching to be sure they are evenly positioned.

flaps & tabs

Flaps and tabs are an interesting addition to children's clothing. Flaps are usually purely decorative, but tabs can also be functional. Adding tabs to shoulder on shirts is a good way of keeping shoulder straps and suspenders in place. When tabs are added to waistbands on skirts and pants, they work to keep belts in place.

1. Flaps are either inserted into a seam or stitched to the surface of the garment. A flap can have any outside shape. Plan the flap with ¼" of seam allowance around the outside edge.

2. Stitch outside edge with right sides together, leaving top open for turning. Turn, trim, and clip if necessary. Press well before attaching to garment.

3. Flaps may also have an inserted-edge trim, or a topstitched trim (see SEWING COLLARS).

4. Tabs are prepared as for flaps, but are generally longer and narrower in shape. Tabs may be inserted into a seam or topstitched in place.

METRIC CONVERSION TABLE (Inches to Centimeters)

Inches		1/16	1/8	1/4	3/8	1/2	5/8	3/4	7/8
		0.16	0.32	0.64	0.95	1.27	1.59	1.91	2.22
1	2.54	2.70	2.86	3.18	3.49	3.81	4.13	4.45	4.76
2	5.08	5.24	5.40	5.72	6.03	6.35	6.67	6.99	7.30
3	7.62	7.78	7.94	8.26	8.57	8.89	9.21	9.53	9.84
4	10.16	10.32	10.48	10.80	11.11	11.43	11.75	12.07	12.38
5	12.70	12.86	13.02	13.34	13.65	13.97	14.29	14.61	14.92
6	15.24	15.40	15.56	15.88	16.19	16.51	16.83	17.15	17.46
7	17.78	17.94	18.10	18.42	18.73	19.05	19.37	19.69	20.00
8	20.32	20.48	20.64	20.96	21.27	21.59	21.91	22.23	22.54
9	22.86	23.02	23.18	23.50	23.81	24.13	24.45	24.77	25.08
10	25.40	25.56	25.72	26.04	26.35	26.67	26.99	27.31	27.62
11	27.94	28.10	28.26	28.58	28.89	29.21	29.53	29.85	30.16
12	30.48	30.64	30.80	31.12	31.43	31.75	32.02	32.39	32.70
13	33.02	33.18	33.34	33.66	33.97	34.29	34.61	34.93	35.24
14	35.56	35.72	35.88	36.20	36.51	36.83	37.15	37.47	37.78
15	38.10	38.26	38.42	38.74	39.05	39.37	36.69	40.01	40.32
16	40.64	40.80	40.96	41.28	41.59	41.91	42.23	42.55	42.86
17	43.18	43.34	43.50	43.82	44.13	44.45	44.77	45.09	45.40
18	45.72	45.88	46.04	46.36	46.67	46.99	47.31	47.63	47.94
19	48.26	48.42	48.58	48.90	49.21	49.53	49.85	50.17	50.48
20	50.80	50.96	51.12	51.44	51.75	52.07	52.39	52.71	53.02
21	53.34	53.50	53.66	53.98	54.29	54.61	54.93	55.25	55.56
22	55.88	56.04	56.20	56.52	56.83	57.15	57.47	57.79	58.10
23	58.42	58.58	58.74	59.06	59.37	59.69	60.01	60.33	60.64
24	60.96	61.12	61.28	61.60	61.91	62.23	62.55	62.87	63.18
25	63.50	63.66	63.82	64.14	64.45	64.77	65.09	65.41	65.72
26	66.04	66.20	66.36	66.68	66.99	67.31	67.63	67.95	68.26
27	68.58	68.74	68.90	69.22	69.53	69.85	70.17	70.49	70.80
28	71.12	71.28	71.44	71.76	72.07	72.39	72.71	73.03	73.34
29	73.66	73.82	73.98	74.30	74.61	74.93	75.25	75.57	75.88
30	76.20	76.36	76.52	76.84	77.15	77.47	77.79	78.11	78.42
31	78.74	78.90	79.06	79.38	79.69	80.01	80.33	80.65	80.96
32	81.28	81.44	81.60	81.92	82.23	82.55	82.87	83.19	83.50
33	83.82	83.98	84.14	84.46	84.77	85.09	85.41	85.73	86.04
34	86.36	86.52	86.68	87.00	87.31	87.63	87.95	88.27	88.58
35	88.90	89.06	89.22	89.54	89.85	90.17	90.49	90.81	91.12
36	91.44	91.60	91.76	92.08	92.39	92.71	93.03	93.35	93.66
37	93.98	94.14	94.30	94.62	94.93	95.25	95.57	95.89	96.20
38	96.52	96.68	96.84	97.16	97.47	97.79	98.11	98.43	98.74
39	99.06	99.22	99.38	99.70	100.01	100.33	100.65	100.97	101.28
40	101.60	101.76	101.92	102.24	102.55	102.87	103.19	103.51	103.82
41	104.14	104.30	104.46	104.78	105.09	105.41	105.73	106.05	106.36
42	106.68	106.84	107.00	107.32	107.63	107.95	108.27	108.59	108.90
43	109.22	109.38	109.54	109.86	110.17	110.49	110.81	111.13	111.44
44	111.76	111.92	112.08	112.40	112.71	113.03	113.35	113.67	113.98
45	114.30	114.46	114.62	114.94	115.25	115.57	115.89	116.21	116.52
46	116.84	117.00	117.16	117.48	117.79	118.11	118.43	118.75	119.06
47	119.38	119.54	119.70	120.02	120.33	120.65	120.97	121.29	121.60
48	121.92	122.08	122.24	122.56	122.87	123.19	123.51	123.83	124.14
49	124.46	124.62	124.78	125.10	125.41	125.73	126.05	126.37	126.68
50	127.00	127.16	127.32	127.64	127.95	128.27	128.59	128.91	129.22
51	129.54	129.70	129.86	130.18	130.49	130.81	131.13	131.45	131.76
52	132.08	132.24	132.40	132.72	133.03	133.35	133.67	133.99	134.30
53	134.62	134.78	134.94	135.26	135.57	135.89	136.21	136.53	136.84
54	137.16	137.32	137.48	137.80	138.11	138.43	138.75	139.07	139.38
55	139.70	139.86	140.02	140.34	140.65	140.97	141.29	141.61	141.92
56	142.24	142.40	142.56	142.88	143.19	143.51	143.83	144.15	144.46
57	144.78	144.94	145.10	145.42	145.73	146.05	146.37	146.69	147.00
58	147.32	147.48	147.64	147.96	148.27	148.59	148.91	149.23	149.54
59	149.86	150.02	150.18	150.50	150.81	151.13	151.45	151.77	152.08
60	152.40	152.56	152.72	153.04	153.35	153.67	153.99	154.31	154.62